On Black Men

On Black Men

David Marriott

EDINBURGH UNIVERSITY PRESS

Edinburgh University Press Ltd
22 George Square, Edinburgh

Typeset in Monotype Apollo
by Norman Tilley Graphics, Northampton,
and printed and bound in Great Britain
by MPG Books Ltd, Bodmin

A CIP record for this book is available
from the British Library

ISBN 0 7486 1017 0 (hardback)
ISBN 0 7486 1016 2 (paperback)

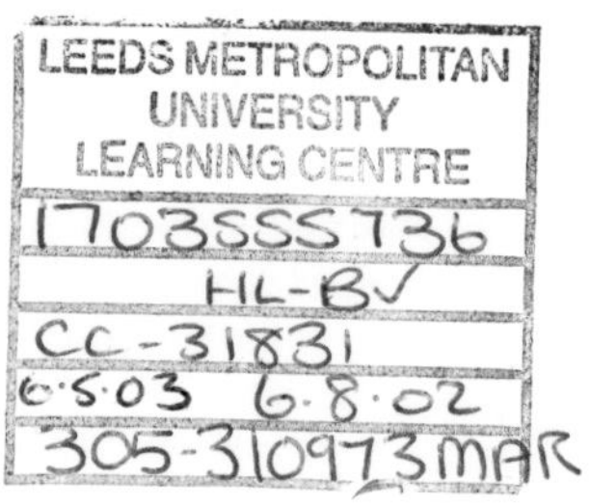

Contents

	List of Illustrations	vi
	Foreword	vii
	Acknowledgements	xvi
I	'I'm gonna borrer me a Kodak': Photography and Lynching	1
II	'Murderous Appetites': Photography and Fantasy	23
III	Black Types	43
IV	Frantz Fanon's War	66
V	Father Stories	95
	Afterword: Either/Or	117
	Works Cited	125
	Index	131

List of Illustrations

1.1 The Lynching of Tom Shipp and Abe Smith at Marion, Indiana, 7 August 1930, by party or parties unknown. Photographs and Prints Division, Schomburg Center for Research in Black Culture, The New York Public Library, Astor, Lenox and Tilden Foundations.

1.2 A lynching in Clanton, Alabama, August 1891. Reprinted from Ida B. Wells-Barnett, *A Red Record* (1895).

1.3 Lynching, Georgia. Reprinted from Richard Wright, *Twelve Million Black Voices: A Folk History of the Negro in the United States of America* (London: Lindsay Drummond, 1947).

2.1 Robert Mapplethorpe, *Man in Polyester Suit* (1980) from *The Black Book* (1986). Copyright © 1980 The Estate of Robert Mapplethorpe.

2.2 Robert Mapplethorpe, *Hooded Man* (1980) from *The Black Book* (1986). Copyright © 1980 The Estate of Robert Mapplethorpe.

6.1 Stephen Lawrence. Copyright © Photo News Service.

Foreword

> For who has not hated his black brother? Simply *because* he is *black, because* he is brother? (James Baldwin, *Nobody Knows My Name*, 1991)

In 1986, the late Joseph Beam, wrote: 'I dare myself to dream' and, 'I dare *us* to dream that we are worth wanting each other' (Beam 1986: 239). *Dare to dream*: a strange watchword, but one that can stand as a coda to this book in its exploration of the symbolic role of black men in the psychic life of culture. But why dreaming? Why daring? As if reality, by itself, were not fatal enough; as if *having* a dream were all we needed to transform ourselves and our futures. Unlike Martin Luther King's famous address on dreams and dreaming – one borne of a conviction, both impossible and necessary, that we dream a just future – Beam's later version seems only halfway hopeful that opening ourselves up to the unexpected can confer a new politics of 'responsibility' (p. 242). But how, asks Richard Wright in *Black Power*, 'could one get the notion that the world could be different if one did not dream?' (Wright 1954: 124). How could one 'strain to feel that which was not yet in existence'? (ibid.: 175). If the longing to dream forms an important part of what shapes the postwar history of African-American men, that syntagm also says something about the politics and experience of dreaming for those black Atlantic men who choose to risk speaking our most secretive languages and desires.

Daring to dream is thus a double commitment to pursue the wished-for risk and revolutionary hope that by dreaming the unthinkable – namely, wanting, rather than hating, one another – we can contest the dreamwork of racist culture in its verisimilitude, address and imagine another kind of *experience*, another kind of living present and future. This book is about the commitment to dream ourselves differently – in literature, psychoanalysis, photography and film – and, in particular, how that dreamwork can start to contest inherited fantasies of black manhood. Indeed, one of the ongoing problems pursued here is how those fantasies that entered our lives so early, so uninvited, so irresistibly, so much in conflict with our pleasures and our freedoms – so relentless in our lived experience – may already be an unwitting part of that dreaming and its future provenance. If our identification with those fantasies produces a fractured doubling of self, how can we distinguish what is interposed from what is properly desired? In fact, if 'the imagination, the imaginary, are only possible to the extent that the real belongs to us', what happens when the real becomes inseparable from an image of black cultural dereliction? (Fanon and Geronimi 1956: 368). When our cultural images are so inhospitable to our dreams and desires? If, as Richard Wright maintains, imagoes of black men cast a 'shadow athwart our national life', for Frantz Fanon the devastating legacy of racism is to be as much part of the dreamlife of the oppressed as of the oppressors (Wright 1983: 39; Fanon 1967). Fanon's insight into how our dreams sustain the dreamwork of culture expresses the kinds of relationships between identity, imago and culture explored in this book. Indeed, if one cannot choose or legislate one's dreaming with respect to either justice or personal longing, do we first need to be free of ourselves, to forget what we have become, for us to redeem our lives as black men?

How then can we hope to dream a reprieve from the real when that real is already a part of our dreaming? These questions alone form the wellspring of my book. Anger has long been a chosen vocation for black men desperate to retain their separatedness, their resistance, to any dream of integration (this angry articulation of self, in turn, a political and aesthetic response to the murderous forms of fantasy ever occupying democracy-in-action). In particular, it is, I think, impossible to separate black men's angry-anxious concern about being reduced to type – black types: imbecilic, oversexed, criminal, murderous, feckless, rapacious – from the many, and conflicting, ways in which black men were and continue to be stereotyped in European and American cultural life. I want to suggest that if, today, black men hate being typecast – there are some words you simply cannot say to us, whether in anger or in jest: a lexical neurosis which, perhaps, precludes the possibility of intimacy – it is because a discourse of types continues to define us in rather predictable ways, even though our occasional conformity to type makes such condescension always possible. (And I'm not talking about a tendency to conform to conformity, either; sometimes habit is nothing more than a cheap congruence of symptoms.)

The transference of white fantasy to black experience, we might say, continues to haunt the black imaginary. James Baldwin once wrote, in *Notes of a Native Son*, that anger and protest were also the irremediable signs of our estrangement: whatever else there is in white America's 'sociological and sentimental image' of the negro, the uneasy suspicion that black men are 'very often playing a part', or better, the idea that black experience is incommunicable and so seldom understood and unaccounted for, is, he argues, unwittingly mirrored in black forms of anger (Baldwin 1964: 18). If America is compelled to rehearse its need 'to reinvest the black face with our guilt', then when we deal in anger, according to Baldwin, we suit our images to that face in the glass. We cannot give our hearts to this demand (be angry!) because anger embodies what we both hate and fear about ourselves; it reenacts the script of a life withheld by self-loathing, a life utterly surprised and confounded by the request 'dare to dream': that is, dare to work over the cultural dreams of black masculinity.

Dare to Dream: '"Look at the nigger! ... Mama, a Negro! ... Hell, he's getting mad ... Mama, the nigger's going to eat me up"', writes Frantz Fanon in *Black Skin, White Masks*, recalling how a young white boy's terror can show up our vulnerability to the dreams, and nightmares, of others. 'My body', he continues, 'was given back to me sprawled out, distorted, recolored, clad in mourning in that white winter day' (Fanon 1967: 113–14). Given back, but 'haemorrhaging' a deplorable quantity of black blood, bleeding from the outside in. If we are unknown to ourselves, we men of colour, it is with good reason. Necessarily strangers to ourselves, we *have* to misunderstand ourselves, estranged from our selves and from each other. For we are *not*. Something smeared. The little French boy's combined fear and anxiety stain Fanon, mark him indelibly both within and without. The overwhelming alienation of the scene – the fear and trembling it engenders – remains traumatic for him. He retains in memory the boy's fear of being eaten, of literally being turned into shit by an organic communion with the black body.

Fanon knows that any black man could have triggered the child's fantasy of being devoured; he knows that he is a type, a black type, who provokes, in white children, white adults, the (unconscious) fear of being consumed by the black other. This is, as Fanon puts it, the 'racial epidermal schema' of Western culture (ibid.: 112). A schema which sustains our images as excessively overpresent and, at the same time, socially invisible. Neither Fanon nor the white boy seems able to avoid this schema, for it is the consequence of a racial hegemony, a fantasy that allows images of whites and blacks to form bonds through racial antagonism. The picture of the black psyche emerging from Fanon's description of this and related incidents is one of 'arriving too late', never on time, violently intruded upon and displaced by racial hatred and phobia that fix him as an imago. Generally, this absorption of the black body into a faecal object is one of the most depressing and melancholic fantasies to ensue from the psychodynamics of intrusion. At the mercy of such images (at once ours and not ours), Fanon presents a picture of the black male psyche as always divided, in conflict with itself. And not only at war, but trapped in a racial drama which is both necessary and unavoidable. Waging rhetorical war on behalf of that psyche, on behalf of black men irrevocably and unforgettably at war with themselves, Fanon's *Black Skin, White Masks* consists, in effect, of multiple fronts and frontiers as the war on the outside crosses over onto the inside, attacking other fronts. At the same time, that war, or wars, is also shown to be inseparable from the aggressions and lynching-hatreds of cultural life. As we shall see, that conflict is central to the various analyses of black male identity put forward in this book.

'The future should be an edifice supported by living men', writes Fanon, and yet 'Man's tragedy, Nietzsche once said, is that he was once a child' (ibid.: 13, 10). This book plots that tragedy through images of dead or murdered black men. Indeed, it begins and ends with men haunted by intrusion and loss, inconsolable in their grief. Interspersed between these is an attempt to describe the versions of reality that are the sources of this suffering. The death of Stephen Lawrence in England, the near-lynching of James Cameron in Marion, Indiana: as different, far apart, and shocking as these events are, the virulence of the responses they provoked, and continue to provoke, is one reason why this book dwells on the real and imaginary disturbances of black male representations in European and North American culture. Representations which invite us to imagine an imitative perversion of human kind, a being incapable of inhibition, morals or ideas; a being whose supernatural indulgence of pleasure and continued satisfaction cannot deal with the contrary of denial or pain; a being whose violent, sexual criminality is incapable of any lasting, or real relationships, only counterfeit, or trickery; a being who remains a perpetual child, rather than a father. The black man is, in other words, everything that the wishful-shameful fantasies of culture want him to be, an enigma of inversion and of hate – and this is our existence as men, as black men.

In 'How Bigger Was Born', Richard Wright describes that enigma in terms of 'an undeveloped negative' whose 'shadowy outlines …

lay in the back of my mind', a negative he needed to bring to light in order to write *Native Son* (Wright 1983: 16, 20). Turning writing into the process for developing negatives, the psyche into a photographic imprint, or type, Wright's use of a photographic metaphor to describe the passage from darkness to light, repression to consciousness, stereotype to literature, allows us to reevaluate the place of photographic images in cultural fantasies of black men. In his search for the histories of that negative, which black men also reflect, Wright had to go against the warnings of a 'mental censor – product of the fears which a Negro feels living in America', fears intimate to his wishes and his dreams, fears which he linked to his inability simply to be a man in America (ibid.: 24). The film negative of black masculinity is, then, also the product of censorship in the wishes and dreamwork of black men. The pressures of that censorship on Wright's desire to write, led him back to his childhood: 'This book, too, goes back to my childhood' (ibid.: 38). Like a dream, perhaps? A dream that dares to speak to and for black men? Crucially, in *Native Son* Wright maps the ties that bind black male wishfulfilment and censorship through the social effects of photography and cinema, and thus brings the question of image and fantasy into dialogue with the massive impact of photography and cinema on black spectators:

> He followed Jack into the darkened movie. The shadows were soothing to his eyes after the glare of the sun. … He moved restlessly, looking around as though expecting to see someone sneaking up on him. …
>
> He looked at *Trader Horn* unfold and saw pictures of naked black men and women whirling in wild dances and heard drums beating and then gradually the African scene changed and was replaced by images in his own mind of white men and women dressed in black and white clothes, laughing, talking, drinking, and dancing. (ibid.: 68, 72)

Images in his own mind: compare this scene with Wright reflecting on a 1953 visit to a Gold Coast movie house in northwestern Africa, as portrayed in *Black Power* (1954):

> The interior was vast, barnlike, undecorated. To find a seat you had to grope your way forward in the dark, bumping into walls and colliding with other people until your hands encountered vacant space. Smoking was allowed and the air was stale. I sat and became aware that an uproar was going on about me and I looked

at the screen to see what was causing it. An advertisement was being projected; a bottle of beer was leaping and jumping on the screen as a British voice extolled its merits … the audience howled with laughter. …

This quality of uproarious detachment continued when the main feature was projected. Indeed, the laughter, the lewd comments, and the sudden shouts rose to such a pitch that I could not hear the shadowy characters say their lines. *I could not follow the story* amid such hubub and came to the conclusion that they could not either; it soon became clear that the story was of minor interest to them. …

During stretches of dialogue, they chatted among themselves about the last explosion of drama, waiting for the action to begin again. It was clear that the African was convinced that movies ought to move. …

Not a little dazed, I made my way back to the hotel and tried to sort out what I had seen and heard. It was quite obvious that the African's time sense was not like our own; it did not *project* forward in anticipation; it oscillated between the present and the past. And at once I knew why there had been no literature in the Gold Coast, no novels or dramas even from those who had been educated in England. …

The African did not strain to feel that which was not yet in existence; he exerted his will to make what had happened happen again. His was a circular kind of time; the past had to be made like the present. Dissatisfaction was not the mainspring of his emotional life; enjoyment of that which he had once enjoyed was the compulsion. (Wright 1954: 172–5; my italics)

Whereas Bigger's distance from the seductive lure of whiteness on screen produces a desire for more, and not less, identification, for Wright the spectacle of African spectators reacting to cinematic images, advertisements and stories throws him into disarray. It is as if Africans are not credulous enough, unable to surrender to the fascination of dream and illusion which cinema (and storytelling) represents. They cannot dream because they cannot project themselves into that trance of relinquishment which true dreaming and true spectatorship warrant. In fact, throughout *Black Power*, Africa and Africans remain, for Wright, an underdeveloped film negative, a censored dream: 'Though the African's whole life was a kind of religious dream, the African scorned the word "dream" … The African takes his religion, which is really a waking *dream*, for reality, and all other dreams are barred, are taboo' (ibid.: 124). One of those barred dreams is clearly cinema, which Wright, in the Gold Coast theatre, connects to a compulsive form of spectatorship. Africans, according to Wright, invest in the repetition of cinematic images via a kind of collective fantasy, and their inability to 'project' and anticipate another existence is compensated by their substitution of cinematic and religious waking dreams for reality.

Wright's anxiety about the proper limits of black spectatorship in relation to the fixated and compensatory racial fantasies of cinema raises a set of persistent questions which will be taken up at different points in this book. 'One of the irreducible dangers to which the moviegoer is exposed', writes James Baldwin in *The Devil Finds Work*, first published in 1976, is 'the danger of surrendering to the corroboration of one's fantasies as they are thrown back from the screen' (Baldwin 1976: 29). Having just remarked that '*no one*', when they go to the movies, '*makes his escape personality black*', he pauses to reflect on how 'the language of the camera is [also] the language of our dreams' (ibid.: 29, 34). At the same time, if 'white Americans have been encouraged to continue dreaming ... black Americans have been alerted to the necessity of waking up' (ibid.: 56–7). Baldwin then concludes: 'it is impossible to pretend that this state of affairs has really altered: a black man, in any case, had certainly best not believe everything he sees in the movies' (ibid.: 57). In *The Devil Finds Work*, then, black men should resist surrendering to what they see in the movies, for what they see are the repeated, and ultimately constraining, images of white peoples' dreams about black men. But can films by black men give us 'better' pictures of our dreams? Should we only surrender to black screens?

For Paul Gilroy, as we shall see, black American Hollywood films of the 1990s reveal a cultural obsession with the figure of the father as a cure for the social disaffection of black brother-sons. These films substitute a paternal dream, he argues, for the real conflicts of black America: class and gender conflicts which cannot be reduced to father–son relations. Like Gilroy, black cultural theory of the past decade has had much to say about the gendering of black nationhood, about the fraternal alliances between black sons in search of their lost fathers. More recently, it has turned its attention to the way that those dreams and desires for a responsible, assertive manhood have self-knowingly excluded the voices of mother-daughters and black gay men from the fraternal bond. But alongside those exclusions, there is another form of exclusion and belonging that interests me: the link between violence, mimesis and the American 'family romance' which supports and lends to that violence its archetypal shape. In each of the chapters that follow I will be arguing that there is an intimate relation between mimetic violence, manhood and dreams of a racial polity. In each case I have chosen black men who seem to me to throw into particular relief, or outline, the question of how cultural and unconscious fantasies of black men as icons, types and antitypes lay claim to particular accounts of the nation-state. The nineteenth-century Episcopalian missionary, Alexander Crummell, will be a central concern here not only because his prophetic dream of civic equality begins with the question: *what value do black men themselves possess as free black men*? but also because, in ways that are eloquent of the problem of identification and representation, he defines black nationality and manhood as imitative assimilations of the characters of others. In charting the vicissitudes of Crummell's thinking on manhood and imitation, we can start by asking what is the link here between a desire to identify, assumed to be already at the root of a drive to copy and assimilate, and the desire to be a black man? Does this lead to white and black identities becoming distorted, imagistic equivalents of one another? A projected screen where phobias and fantasies meet?

Acting as both a limit and provocation to dreams of white selfhood, it becomes evident that there is a demand that black men perform a script – become interchangeable with the uncanny, deeply unsettling, projections of culture. The legacy of that demand on black male identity not only works to sustain a repertoire of relationships between black men, imago and cultural fantasy, but continues to have a distorting, and necessarily violent, effect on how black men learn to see themselves and one another. Hung by our dreaming, then, blinded by the dreams of culture: *On Black Men* begins with an exploration of the inverse relation between negative and image, looking and desire; how white fears and desires slice like a knife through the eyes of petrified black men, through the innermost recesses of our being. From the public spectacle of lynchings to the private dramas of erotic consumption, lynching scenes to 'art' images of black male nudes, what is revealed is a vicious pantomime of unvarying reification and compulsive fascination, of whites taking a look at themselves through images of black desolation, of blacks intimately dispossessed by that selfsame looking. In this sense, one of the aims of this book is to assess the disfiguring impact of those imagoes – internalised, they will haunt black men for the rest of their lives – and their effects on our unconscious beliefs and desires.

Finally, what follows can be read as a series of fragments collated tentatively, uncertainly, on the relations between race and psychoanalysis. In 'The Fire Next Time', James Baldwin writes: 'One can give nothing whatever without giving oneself – that is to say, risking oneself. If one cannot risk oneself, then one is simply incapable of giving' (Baldwin 1998: 336). Giving, like dreaming, then, becomes an art of risk for some black men. And yet, if racism, as Fanon intimates, brings dreaming to a halt, can dreaming ever save us? And what, psychoanalytically speaking, would it mean to risk ourselves knowing that the contempts of culture are already inside us, part of those painful unpleasures confounding our experiences as black men? To live with hatred as our most intimate possession becomes, then, the truly difficult task of our dreams.

Acknowledgements

Parts of a number of these chapters have been published in earlier versions: material from Chapters 1 and 2 appear as 'Bordering On: the Black Penis', in Lindsay Smith and Alan Sinfield (eds), *Textual Practice*. Chapter 3 was given as a seminar 'On Black Types' at the University of Sussex Graduate Colloquium (1998). The brief discussion of Fanon and Lacan in Chapter 4 is abridged from 'Bonding Over Phobia', in Christopher Lane (ed.), *The Psychoanalysis of Race* (New York: Columbia University Press, 1998). Parts of Chapter 5 appear as 'In Memory of Absent Fathers' in Jan Campbell and Janet Harbord (eds), *Psycho-Politics and Cultural Desires* (London: UCL Press, 1998). I wish to thank the editors of these books and journal, both for inviting me to publish and for permission to reuse the material. In all cases, the earlier versions have been substantially revised and expanded.

I am also grateful to a large number of people in various universities who, by invitation to present work-in-progress, allowed progress to occur. Let me mention in particular Christopher Lane, Phil Cohen, Roland François Lack, Michael Temple, Peter Middleton, Vicky Lebeau, Christine Clegg, Hazel Carby, Jacqueline Rose, Alan Sinfield, Adam Philips, Michael Hanchard, Andrew Crozier and Mandy Merck. But the study also owes debts that cannot be more specifically acknowledged to colleagues and students at Queen Mary and Westfield College, the University of Sussex, University of Wisconsin-Milwaukee, the University of Southampton, as well as the Hayward Gallery and the Tavistock Institute. Vicky Lebeau read the manuscript through with her customary critical acumen; I wish to thank her for her many insights and criticisms.

I was the beneficiary of an Arts Humanities Board grant in 1999, which gave me time to complete my research. This book also derives directly from my teaching, in particular my graduate seminar on 'Fanon', which I have taught for a number of years at Queen Mary and Westfield College, and which has helped me to pursue and clarify the ideas presented here.

Finally, I am grateful to my editor, Jackie Jones, for her support and patience.

Brighton, 1999

1 'I'm gonna borrer me a Kodak': Photography and Lynching

A hot August night in Marion, Indiana. 1930. Accused of rape and murder, a young black man stands – a bloody mass – on the courthouse lawn. There's a noose around his neck. The mob surrounds him: thousands of people baying. Above him, the bodies of Thomas Shipp and Abram Smith hang from the trees. 'In my mind', writes James Cameron, years later, in 1982, 'I was already dead' (Cameron 1995: 10).

Already dead? A few hours before, Cameron had seen his two friends mauled to death. Shipp and Smith. Shipp first, beaten with fists and clubs and stones by a crowd that, Cameron tells us, comes to life at the sight of Tommy's body. 'It was terrifying and sickening to watch', he recalls, 'yet I couldn't turn my eyes away' (ibid.: 60). Gaze riveted, Cameron watches Thomas, beaten and dragged senseless, come back from the dead – 'he fought the mob, savagely, for a few seconds' – in time to die: 'The rope, looped through the bars of the window did the rest' (ibid.: 61). The crowd – some fifteen thousand people – frenzy, drawn to the sight of blood. Pushing and shoving to get 'a closer look at the "dead nigger"', a souvenir of bloody spectacle. 'Murderous appetite' is how Cameron describes it, while the crowd begins chanting for 'another nigger' (ibid.).

This time it's Abram Smith. Another black body, torn and bleeding, a crowbar rammed through his chest. More hunting for souvenirs: while Abe and Tommy hang lifeless from the trees, the mob – screaming now, and giggling – take out their Kodaks. 'As other mob members took pictures of the spectacle', Cameron writes, 'they vied with one another to have their pictures taken alongside the tree showing the bodies of Abe and Tommy swaying in the breeze' (ibid.: 63). Click, smile, click – and then the crowd heads back towards the jail. It's Cameron's turn.

The black prisoners in Cameron's cell are waiting with him. They can hear the mobsters coming up the stairs, 'a jamming bunch of violent, ruthless, Black-hating white men' (ibid.: 65). They're chanting for Cameron – 'To think they wanted me that bad!' – but the ringleaders don't know what he looks like. They have to find him out. A terrible scene: black prisoners, crawling for their lives ('Don't hang us Mister Bossman!') while others, defiant, hold Cameron back. Finally, 'Dere he is!': one black prisoner – an old man, in jail with his son – points Cameron out. 'A novel scene', he concludes. 'To them, this was a sight that every white person in the world should be able to witness. What a spectacle' (ibid.: 65–71).

What happens next may be a miracle. Running the gauntlet of the crowd (the Marion Police clear a path through the swarm), Cameron is pounded, bitten, spat on: 'A pick handle crashed down against the side of my head' (ibid.: 72). His head in a noose, he passes out. 'I was already dead', he says, again. 'With the noose around my neck and death in my brain, I waited for the end' (ibid.: 73, 74). And then he hears the voice. 'It was a feminine voice, sweet, clear, but unlike anything I had ever heard', Cameron writes, still wondering at a voice – echo-like, as if from a long way off – which came to intervene in his fate: '"**Take this boy back. He had nothing to do with any raping or killing!**" That was all the voice said' (ibid.: 74). That was all. But what happens next is stranger still:

> Abruptly, impossibly, silence fell over that raging mob, as if they had been struck dumb. No one moved or spoke a word. I stood there in the midst of thousands of people, and as I looked at the mob around me I thought I was in a room, a large room where a photographer had strips of film negatives hanging from walls to dry. I couldn't tell whether the images on the film were white or Black, they were simply mobsters captured on film, surrounding me everywhere I looked. Time stood still for that one instant. The fury of that mob had been quelled in the moment.
>
> A brief eternity passed as I stood there as if hypnotized. Then the roomful of negatives disappeared and I found myself looking into the faces of people who had been flat only moments ago. (ibid.)

Some fifty years later, when Cameron came to record the events of that night, he interviewed hundreds of people who claimed to be part of the crowd. 'Not one of them said they heard that voice', he writes. 'Their explanation usually was, "You were just lucky!"' (ibid.: 75). Lucky? Miraculous? Who can know. After all, as Cameron tells it in 1982, he experienced that night through the vision of an image-making process: the technical production of the photograph which becomes one way to live through the real on 7 August 1930.

Hypnotised by a room full of negatives, it is as if time stands still for Cameron: the moment impressed and – later – straining to return (the negative from which the image will be cut and *developed*). The mob, stilled by a voice, have their images taken and 'hung' up to dry; Cameron's experience of the lynch mob is recalled in terms of mobsters captured on film. The photographer and his negative still and freeze the moment (like the voice holding off death). That is, Cameron's vision seems to support a (vengeful) fantasy of watching the mobsters hang from the walls: the curious coincidence between the work of photography and the work of lynching. To survive – the subtitle of Cameron's book is 'A Survivor's Story' – is to immerse oneself in photographic representation. Re-presentation is what brings the spectacle of injury and death to an end. That representation, like the voice, continues to haunt him: 'I can still hear it sometimes' (ibid.). Voice and image still time, silence the crowd, freeze Cameron's vision on the negatives: the black and white images of the mob which are his experience of trauma.

Apparently, the crowd drew back, 'with shame in their eyes', Cameron notes (ibid.: 75). The hands that had beaten him and put the noose around his neck became gentle, removing the rope, drawing back, until Cameron finds himself alone under the tree. Bruised, bleeding, he made his way, unaided, back to the jail. The crowd cannot look now: 'Their gazes invariably dropped when their eyes met mine' (ibid.). The mobsters obeying a command which, it seems, only Cameron heard: let him be.

The next day, 8 August 1930, Cameron is on his way from Huntington, the nearby town to which – for his own safety – he had been taken over night. He's face down on the floor of a police car but he can hear the voices of the newsboys selling their papers: 'Read all about it! Mob lynches two Negroes here last night! Read all about it! Extra! Extra! Extra!' (ibid.: 84).

The day before, rumours of a lynch mob had been front-page news (details of the Marion lynching were broadcast over the radio throughout the Midwest). Now the papers are carrying scenes of the lynching they had advertised – and, once again, Cameron is forced to look. Telling him to 'take a look at the news', one of his jailers thrusts a newspaper into Cameron's face. 'On the front page', Cameron recalls, 'was a picture of Tommy and Abe with ropes around their necks, swinging from the limbs of a tree. Below them were many upturned faces, pointing and laughing at the spectacle' (ibid.: 84).

A spectacle, one that blurs Cameron's vision with anger, fuels his rage against 'every white person in the world' – as if the circulation

1.1 The Lynching of Tom Shipp and Abe Smith at Marion, Indiana, 7 August 1930, by party or parties unknown. Photographs and Prints Division, Schomburg Center for Research in Black Culture, The New York Public Library, Astor, Lenox and Tilden Foundations.

of the photograph universalises the violence, and racism, of the lynch mob across the white community. And turns Cameron himself into a 'one-man mob inside. I wanted to kill a white man! Any white man would do!' (ibid.: 85). That rage is part of the power of an image which preserves not only the horror of the black men's bodies – a horror which Cameron is forced to see again as the detectives drive past the hanging tree – but the pleasure of the mob: grinning, pointing, challenging Cameron and, by extension, any black man who has to look at this image. Why *show* Cameron that photo? Or, more precisely, what does that showing tell us about the positioning of the black man as both victim and spectator – spectator as victim – of lynching in a racist culture? Could Cameron look at that image without seeing himself? (He was, I think, supposed to see himself: let's not underestimate the sadism generating, and generated by, the killing of black men.) Can any black man resist the identification with a dead black body written into an image which reproduces the divisions of racist culture by showing white men pointing and laughing? At that point, I would suggest, the identification can be irresistible.

To read James Cameron's *A Time of Terror*, first published in 1982, is to take on a terrible, and fantasmatic, legacy. It is not only that the history of lynching in the United States is one that black men are forced to engage (that history is central to the various chapters of this book); but, as a black man who survived the scene of lynching, who lived to tell his own story, Cameron is a rare figure in that history: a voice echoing across the decades, come to haunt his readers as he himself remains haunted by the 'echo-like' voice which saved him so many years ago. Is it possible? Do I believe him? The sound of that voice – whose? Cameron's? – carries the desperate imaginings of more than half a century, imprinting itself on his awareness like a photographic plate. Crucial to Cameron's role in contemporary African-American attempts to tell a story which has not been told, voice and image are also central to the event which has to become story – the voice which only Cameron hears, the photographs which, as I want to show, come to play a key part in the history, and experience, of lynching in the United States.

There are numerous images of black men, tortured and lynched; sometimes there are white faces with tin smiles, gawping up at them. Countless stories woven around the scenes. There to frighten, to show black men their future, such images document the truth of lynching as both trauma and gala: a show *for* the white men, women and children before whom it is staged. 'A vacant shoe, an empty tie, a ripped shirt, a lonely hat, and a pair of trousers stiff/ with black blood': Richard Wright, in 'Between the World and Me', first published in 1935, pursues the body destroyed in the course of such festivity: 'And upon the trampled grass were buttons, dead matches, butt-ends of cigars and/ cigarettes, peanut shells, a drained gin-flask, and a whore's lipstick' (Wright 1935). Smoking, drinking, eating, sexing, the crowd looked on the scene of a black man's body tarred, feathered, burned: 'Scattered traces of tar, restless arrays of feathers, and the lingering smell of/ gasoline' (ibid.).

Cameron describes the sickness which overwhelms him at the sight of the image of his dead friends; Wright recalls his mind 'frozen with a cold pity for the life that was gone' when he comes across the debris of a public lynching (Cameron 1995: 84; Wright 1935). Nausea, petrification: nothing like the gleam in the white man's eye as he vies with his neighbour to have his picture taken. Part of the rites (or rights) of lynching, photographs of dead black men and their white executioners are meant to be seen. They are *public* portraits: posed, compelling, an exhibition and narration of racist violence. Pressed up close, or drawing back, the camera lens is a means to fashion the self through the image of a dead black man – and, sometimes, to identify with the white men, and women, at the scene. Spectacle, and gallery, both: a consolidation of racist community and a posture of whiteness. Consider, for example, the repertoire of poses on display at the lynching in Clanton, Alabama in August 1891.

Published in Ida B. Wells-Barnett's *A Red Record*, in 1895, this image is arranged, orderly, composed – a far cry from the hectic jostling described by Cameron. The assembly of (largely) white men and boys look out at the photographer/spectator – as if they have sated their appetites for looking at the black corpse hanging above them (only one or two still look up). What they want to see now is themselves looking at the camera: judges and executioners in the lives, and deaths, of black men. Above all, they are vigilant. An image of white identity emerges from a spectacle of annihilation: the lynchers posing, grimly, alongside their black 'trophies'. A moment frozen in time, flash-lit in the heat of subsided passion.

That compulsion to bring the eye of the camera up close, to put themselves in the picture as spectators of torn black flesh, means that we – black men – can still look at those lynchers: look at them looking at teeth, nails, bone, skin. What are they thinking about as they gaze out at the camera, pointing up at black bodies dangling in the trees? Sullen, stern, defiant, satisfied, curious: what do they see? What do they want us to see? That, as Richard Wright puts it in a brief comment on another such image, 'the law is white' (Wright 1947: 44)?

Wright will come to use the photographic evidence of lynching to present his own convictions about the spectacular place of black men in white scopic pleasure: 'the law is white'. And if this is law, it is both fantasmatic and perverse. Consider, for example, the following account given by Howard Kester in *The Lynching of Claude Neal* in 1934: 'After taking the nigger to the woods ... they cut off his penis. He was made to eat it. Then they cut off his testicles and made him eat them and say he liked it' (Kester 1934, cited in Dowd Hall 1984: 339). As a response to the 'unspeakable crime' of black-on-white rape, the act of forcing a man to 'fuck' himself to death with his own excised genitals, to feed and gorge himself on his own violating (violated) pleasure, may well have been hugely satisfying to those assembled – especially when the man got to confess his (seeming) enjoyment. To hear him desire his own death – and so turn their terrible pleasure into his own violent wish – was to construct a vision of the castrated black man as one actively seeking

1.2 A lynching in Clanton, Alabama, August 1891. Reprinted from Ida B. Wells-Barnett, *A Red Record* (1895).

1.3 Lynching, Georgia. Reprinted from Richard Wright, *Twelve Million Black Voices: A Folk History of the Negro in the United States of America* (London: Lindsay Drummond, 1947).

the pleasures of castration. And what of the black man's desires and identifications here? It must have been exhausting trying to name that pleasure, to mention – without choking – how much he liked that severed penis now become his new protruding tongue.[1] I suppose that this little bit of theatre serves to reveal, and support, a race hatred predicated on an identification between blackness and sexual guilt, an identification which generates the sadistic desire to witness the spectacle – the stench – of emasculated black men slowly bleeding to death. As such, it is a law which operates through visual terror. The lesson to be learned through the murderous gazes of these white men is that you might be reduced to something that 'don't look human' – a reduction which is, precisely, your annihilation and their pleasure. In *Red Wine First*, published in 1947, Nedra Tyre records the thoughts of one Skinny Slaton: 'Well, said Skinny Slaton, shore as I'm born I'm gonna borrer me a kodak tomorrer and I'm coming back here and I'm gonna take me some pitchers of that. Don't look human, does it?' (Tyre 1947: 112–13).

The technological moment which gives us the Kodak – the first turn-of-the-century mass-produced roll-film camera – also gives us a way of venturing into some dark places. For Slaton, anxious to go borrow a Kodak, the photograph represents the climax of an unfolding drama. More than an aid to memory (though it is that too), the photograph is a part of the process, another form of racist slur which can travel through time to do its work: 'Don't look human, does it?' No doubt, Slaton is fascinated by what taking the picture can do and reveal about himself: a figure in a public event, a means to fashion the self through the image of a dead black man and the identification with fellow whites which can follow. At the same time, it is as if he wants to make an archive of what he sees, to preserve an event for the benefit of those who could not be there (friends, family, a son or daughter, perhaps). Wish you were here. A grotesque family album. Slaton wants others to see him there, to know he was present at the obliteration of a man whose end could not be imagined without this visible prop. Who can deny the (merciless) evidence of such a photo, its framing – and containing – of the stink of the real?

To put this another way: white men, and women, demand a keepsake, a *memento mori*: toes, fingers, or – most highly prized – a black penis, a black scrotum. 'Miller's body hung thus exposed from three to five o'clock', writes Ida B. Wells-Barnett in *A Red Record* in 1895, 'during which time, several photographs of him as he hung dangling at the end of the chain were taken, and his toes and fingers cut off' (Wells-Barnett 1991: 182). But how long will they keep, these organs and limbs, subject to the reek of putrefaction? They're not like the image, which registers a moment in time complete, pure, clean – free of the blood, and rot, of the lost body part. Reining in the spill of human wreckage, reviving the carnival atmosphere of the day, the photograph is there to be gazed at, and fingered, over and over again: Look at me. I was there.

Again, it was all part of the ritual: this *appetite* for document, this devouring by the eye – as if only a camera can bring the spectator close enough for the eye to be embedded in flesh. And, of course, the camera plays its part in sustaining that appetite, prolonging the scene it is supposed to record. 'After three full hours had been spent in torturing the two', writes Sutton Griggs in *The Hindered Hand* in 1905, 'the spokesman announced that they were now ready for the final act. The brother of Sidney Fletcher was called for and was given a match. He stood near his mutilated victims *until the photographer could take a picture of the scene*' (Griggs 1905: 133–4; my italics). The final act in a popular melodrama: the camera itself – the drive to document, to be in the show – becomes part of that drama, prolonging the agony of the mutilated blacks who must hope that death will come quickly. From the first act – the moment of accusation: rape, murder, theft – this is what the audience has been waiting for: confirmation, via a fatal iconography of the brute black male, that he really 'don't look human'.[2]

How do we look at these pictures now? How do we start to try to understand the hatred, and misery, on display through them? We know now – as we knew then – that most of the charges on which black men were 'tried' by Judge Lynch (to coin Ida B. Wells' well-known phrase) were fabricated; they were ideological narratives, or fantasies, of black men as murderers, rapists, thieves: 'the black brute ... lurking in the dark' (Dowd Hall 1984: 344). In other words, the act of lynching is part of a racial imaginary, a primal scene of racist culture in the southern states of America, in which black men bear the brunt of a hatred which seems, at times, to know no bounds.[3] Burdened by history, black men lived, and perhaps continue to live, in that climate, one permeated by racist fantasy – and the violence to which it so often gives rise. As Wright was one of the first to point out in *Black Boy*, first published in 1945, you don't have to see a lynching to live with its effects: 'I had never in my life been abused by whites, but I had already become as conditioned to their existence as though I had been the victim of a thousand lynchings' (Wright 1945: 84).

'The victim of a thousand lynchings'? On Wright's reading the black man can die and die and die again – as if, as I suggested before, the identification between the black man looking and the black man lynched becomes irresistible. That identification can, in Wright's work, run riot through the black man's psychic and cultural life. Describing his response to the story of a black woman whose husband had been 'seized and killed by a mob', Wright insists on the 'emotional truth' of the feeling that 'there existed men against whom I was powerless, men who could violate my life at will' (the pedagogic value of the lynch photo/plot) (ibid.: 83–4). He doesn't know if the story is true or not, but it keeps him awake at nights: taking the place of his dreams, the lynching scene becomes a daytime nightmare. Relief comes only with the young Wright's resolve to 'emulate' the black woman who, concealing a rifle at her husband's funeral, shot dead four of his attackers. Revenge, defence, attack: a refusal to accept 'their cruelty as the law of my life' (ibid.: 84). But Wright knows the limits of *that* identification, one that has no 'objective value'. 'My spontaneous fantasies lived in my mind', he continues, 'because I felt completely helpless in the face of this threat that might come upon me at any time, and because there did not exist to my knowledge any possible course of action which could have saved me if I had ever been confronted by a white mob' (ibid.). No possible action, so Wright needs (and it is *need* rather than, say, wish) his defensive fantasy, his way of defending himself psychically against the death of a thousand lynchings. But no defence, either, because Wright knows that this fantasy has no 'objective value': it cannot be made *real*, unlike the racist fantasy which structures reality for both whites and blacks.

Above all, Wright's exploration of his experience of white Southern culture uncovers an identification with, or interpellation by, what he – a black man – imagines white desire to be: 'Even when a white man asked us an innocent question', Wright recalls in *Twelve Million Black Voices*, first published in 1941,

> some unconscious part of us would listen closely, not only to the obvious words, but also to the intonations of voice that indicated what kind of answer he wanted; and, automatically, we would determine whether an affirmative or negative reply was expected, and we would answer, not in terms of objective truth, but in terms of what the white man wanted to hear. (Wright 1941: 41)

Imagine the black man the white man wants you to be, then, and be him (or, at least, mime him). To push the point, our unconscious – or some of it, in Wright's terms – is given over to that work of second-guessing, of dare and double dare. There's no place here for what the black man wants, or for a black unconscious driven by its own desire and aggression. On the contrary. The unconscious (if that is what it is) is taken over, usurped, by the work of identifying (with) what the white man wants.

Even if the black man is a dead man, a lynched man? We can start to clarify this through one of the key works on race, hatred and fantasy: Frantz Fanon's *Black Skin, White Masks*, first published in French in 1952, translated into English in 1967. Towards the end of *Black Skin, White Masks*, Fanon describes his book as a 'mirror' in whose reflective image black men can view their own future. 'This book, it is hoped', he writes in 'The Negro and Psychopathology', 'will be a mirror with a progressive infrastructure, in which it will be possible to discern the Negro on the road to disalienation' (Fanon 1967: 184). A new image in the mirror is, for Fanon, crucial if that disalienation is to take place: black men need to look, and be reflected, *otherwise*, to become other than the distorted and fantasmatic image of white desire. Imagine a 'mirror of confusion' (to use James Baldwin's phrase) in which only the shade, or shadow, of the black man can appear. An image of hate, a hated image. A phobic imago, to use Fanon's terms. Listen, for example, to his account of the psycho-social dynamics of Negrophobogenesis: 'Is the Negro's [sexual] superiority real? Everyone *knows* that it is not. But that is not what matters. The prelogical thought of the phobic has decided that such is the case' (ibid.: 159).

It is the triumph, and complexity, of Fanon's thinking that he was able to identify the inner life of specular confusion supporting the knot of phobic fantasy. For Fanon, the problem is that white phobic anxiety about black men takes the form of a fetishistic investment in their sexuality: crudely, being well-hung, the black man must be hung well. In other words, the violated body of the black man comes to be used as a defence against the anxiety, or hatred, that body appears to generate. Describing that basic ambivalence as 'negrophobia', Fanon uses the syntax of fetishism – 'I know, but all the same' – to account for the construction of the black man as phobic object: 'Everyone knows that he is not superior, but all the same ...'. But, again, what of black men in all this? What, if anything, can be glimpsed *of them* in these alienating, and confusing, images? What do black men see when they encounter, perhaps for the first time, a phobic image of themselves in (white) culture?

In *Black Skin, White Masks*, we find once again the spectacle of a lynching that the black child hasn't *seen* but which, in some sense, appears to have happened to him. 'Frequently', Fanon argues in 'The Negro and Psychopathology',

> the negro who becomes abnormal [*s'anormalise*] has never had any relations with the White man. Has there been an ancient experience and repression in the unconscious [*Y a-t-il eu expérience ancienne et refoulement dans l'inconscient?*]? Has the young black child seen his father beaten or lynched by the white man? Has there been a real traumatism [*traumatisme effectif*]? To all this we have to answer: *no*. Well then? (Fanon 1952: 118; 1967: 145; t.m.)

Well then? What has traumatised this black child who has not *seen* his father beaten or lynched? Fanon's statement on what the black child has seen, or not, implies that the child has been caught looking not by the real but by his own racist imaginary, a capture inseparable from an exposure to the cultural representations of the 'white world'. But what if the cultural milieu of that white world insists that the child's eye zone in on such real traumas as a way of grounding its – racist culture's – own fantasy? Which it did. What if the cultural traffic in *images* of the black man as phobic object – beaten, disfigured, lynched – is trauma enough? As Vicky Lebeau has pointed out in a recent discussion of *Black Skin, White Masks*, that insight – the trauma of representation – is, in fact, central to Fanon's analysis of the black child *devouring* [*dévoré*] and identifying with the stories and images of white culture. Brought up to think and act subjectively 'like a white man' (Fanon's phrase), Lebeau suggests that:

> the black man who encounters himself as a phobic object within white culture encounters the dereliction of his *own* self-representation through that culture: dereliction as one of the effects of a hatred coming now from both inside and outside, which Fanon tracks throughout *Black Skin, White Masks*. (Lebeau 1998: 115)

If Fanon seems impervious to the invasive possibilities of real, racial violence in that child's neurotic encounter, blind to the extent to which that evil twin lurking in the mirror of culture may prove to be more than a dark, imaginary double, it is worth taking a few moments to think about how this accusation squares with his continued insistence on the violence of the real. As a symbol of the self-destructive, lacerating ground upon which phobia and fantasy meet, the black child, in taking up the burden of such imagery, Fanon concludes, has been fatally exposed to the glare of those phobic anxieties constructed upon his visual image – as have other blacks exposed, for the first time, to the colonial fantasies of European culture. This vision of blacks confounded by their reflected images is also acutely – powerfully – aware of the collusions between unconscious and cultural forms of violence; 'of a dreaming possessed not, or not only, by the subject's own wishful-shameful fantasies but by the real' (Lebeau 1998: 121). Not only is the 'sadistic aggression' [*agressivité sadique*] of culture most visibly at work in the child's 'sacrificial dedication [*oblativité*]' to his distorted image; his unconscious dreamlife has learned to play its part by demanding that debasement (Fanon 1967: 147). There is, in other words, a remarkable correlation between the imago – the fantasy – of black men in cultural life and black self-images. Behind those images and inverted screens lurks a dark intruder albeit framed by a black (and white) vision of black identity; an imago stalking a little black child through his memories and dreams.

'I have never seen a lynching', writes Calvin Hernton in his now classic *Sex and Racism in America* in 1969, 'never looked upon a Negro who has been castrated. I understand, however, and *know*, that it is a terrible sight' (Hernton 1969: 100). That understanding, and knowledge, comes not only from photographs and stories but from those who *have* seen – like the man who recollects a lynching in Mississippi, Alabama which took place when he was nine years old. Let's listen to the account he gives to Hernton. 'I will never forget it', he says:

> I can still see him hanging up like that. ... The next morning my uncle and me and me and some other coloured folks in the county went to look at the man who had been lynched. The man's wife and brother were with us, and they were crying. Everybody was afraid. I wasn't – for I really didn't know what to expect. But maybe I was a little scared just because of all the racket that went on that night. Anyway, when we got there in the woods, everyone started crying and turning their heads away in horror. I looked up at the man. I knew him, yet he was so messed up I could not tell who he was. He was naked, and they had put tar on him and burnt him. He smelled awful. Then I saw what they had done. Even though I was only nine, I knew what they had done was a sin. They had cut out his private and left it laying on the ground. The blood had caked all about his legs and thighs. (ibid. 1969: 100)

This is what the lynchers want. A memory, an imago, that will not go away. Not only the body, burned and stinking in the trees, but black men, women and children looking, and then looking away, from what the white men have done. 'Everybody was afraid' except the young black boy who, not knowing what to expect, keeps looking until he can see what has happened. Something has been torn away and left lying on the ground, something private which confirms – as, it seems, the tarred body cannot – that what has happened is a 'sin'. It's a vision which stays with this boy for the rest of his life – 'I can still see him hanging up like that' – a reminder of how fragile his possession of himself, his 'manhood', can be. The real difference between black and white men. 'Psychologically, he [the black male] experiences himself as castrated', writes Hernton in the course of a discussion of 'The Negro Male': a castration which, in the context of African-American history, suggests the impact of the real on that psychology, the psychic weight of learning what to expect by going down to the woods (ibid.: 59). The lesson will stay with you: blackness afflicted, mutilated, a fatal way of being alive.[4]

You might end up wishing you were white. That you were one of the white children playing around the smoking body of a black man, a happy part of the show. The participation of white children at lynchings is documented in photographs and in reports like the following from the *New York Times* in 1899:

> All the afternoon children, some of them not more than six years old, kept up the fire around the blackened body by throwing grass, brush, bits of boards, and everything combustible that they could get together. This they kept up until dark ...[5]

Inexhaustible, excited, these children can play till dark, part of the type of 'racket' which so frightened the black man interviewed by Hernton. Their presence – so difficult to separate from an idea of innocence, of not knowing – takes us back to the question of where does white hatred come from? What does it have to do with this play? Is this a game played in deadly seriousness, a miming of their parents' own excitement, a search for their loving approval: 'Look at me, I'm burning the black man ... for you'? Are these children spellbound by their parents' own fascinated looking? What do these white men and women want their children to see and to think? What's the purpose of the 'lesson' when it is directed not, or not only, at a black boy but at a white one?

James Baldwin's remarkable short story, *Going to Meet the Man*, first published in 1965, is aimed directly at that question. Race, sexuality, violence: these are the crucial terms of Baldwin's exploration of a white man's memory of a lynching which took place in his hometown when he was eight years old. By now the scene will be familiar. It was, Baldwin writes, 'like a Fourth of July picnic'; 'His father said, "We're going on a picnic. You won't ever forget *this* picnic –!"' (Baldwin 1965: 244, 245). At least, that's how Deputy Sheriff Jesse recalls it, years later, lying in bed next to his wife, Grace. As the story opens, Jesse is trying and failing to make love to Grace. 'He could not ask her to do just a little thing for him', Baldwin writes obliquely, 'just to help him out, just for a little while, the way he could ask a nigger girl to do it' (ibid.: 231). The reader is left to wonder what that 'little thing' might be, at the same time as Baldwin draws attention to the race-ing of sexual difference, the sexual violence which is a central part of black women's experience in the southern states of America, the image of a black girl which passes between the white man and his wife. '"Go to sleep," she said, gently, "you've got a hard day tomorrow"' (ibid.: 231).

A hard day to come for any Sheriff of a southern town at the height of the black Civil Rights demonstrations and voter-registration drives. Take Sheriff Clark in Selma, Alabama, for example – a man who 'cannot be dismissed as a total monster', as Baldwin puts it in his brief essay, 'The American Dream and the American Negro', also published in 1965. 'I'm sure he loves his wife and children', writes Baldwin, 'and likes to get drunk ... but he does not know what drives him to use the club, to menace with the gun and to use the cattle prod' (Baldwin 1998: 716). Reading across from this article, which first appeared in *The New York Times Magazine*, to *Going to Meet the Man*, it is clear that Baldwin's fiction is in complex dialogue with his political journalism on the struggle for black civic equality: segregation, voter rights, and non-violent demonstrations. In fact, Sheriff Clark appears to be the model, or starting-point, for Jesse whose stream of consciousness drives the long night of this story. Lying awake listening for the first sounds of dawn, Jesse, Deputy Sheriff for seven years, can't get it up. What's keeping him down – 'He tried again; he wretchedly failed again. Then he just lay there, silent, angry, and helpless' (ibid.: 231) – and awake is the thought of those 'black stinking coons': the 'liver-lipped students' (the civil rights demonstrators) who would be outside the court-house tomorrow: 'those black breasts *leap* against the *leaping* cattle prod' (ibid.: 231, 232, 233). Like Sheriff Clark, Jesse has been cattle prodding a woman's breasts, the memory of which calls to mind how he'd 'felt himself violently stiffen – with no warning at all' while cattle prodding a black male Civil Rights worker earlier that morning (ibid.: 237). Listening to his wife's breathing in the dark, feeling the limp weight of his body, the scene in the cell stirs a half-remembered, half-forgotten memory of his parents. After all, he'd felt that dreadful pleasure before. 'It had been night, as it was now, he was in the car between his mother and his father, sleepy, his head in his mother's lap, sleepy, and yet full of excitement' (ibid.: 242). He could hear the negroes singing across the fields. '"I guess they singing for him," his father said, seeming very weary and subdued now' (ibid.).

Tired, wondering and yet knowing about *him* – a black man on the run from the lynch mob – Jesse's thoughts turn to his black friend, Otis. 'They wrestled together in the dirt. Now the thought of Otis made him sick' (ibid.: 242). He hadn't seen Otis that morning:

> 'No,' said his father, 'I reckon Otis's folks was afraid to let him show himself this morning.'
>
> 'But Otis didn't do nothing!' now his voice sounded questioning.
>
> 'Otis *can't* do nothing,' said his father, 'he's too little.'
>
> The car lights picked up their wooden house, which now solemnly approached them, the lights falling around it like yellow dust. Their dog, chained to a tree, began to bark.
>
> 'We just want to make sure Otis *don't* do nothing,' said his father, and stopped the car. He looked down at Jesse. 'And you tell him what your daddy said, you hear?'
>
> 'Yes, sir,' he said. (ibid.: 243)

You tell Otis. But what? From father to son to black boy, the message passes on. At first obscure – Jesse is still questioning – that message will be burned into Jesse's consciousness by the burning of a black man's body. And it will change forever his childhood love for Otis.

Just as it changes the relationship between white man and wife. Lying in bed that night Jesse overhears the intimacy of his parents, his 'mother's moan, his father's sigh', and, finally, the frightening presence of his 'father's breathing [which] seemed to fill the world' (ibid.: 243). That sexual pleasure as if in preparation for the 'pleasures' of the following day: the lynching scene which is the climax, the horror, of *Going to Meet the Man*:

> He watched his mother's face. Her eyes were very bright, her mouth was open: she was more beautiful than he had ever seen her, and more strange. He began to feel a joy he had never felt before. He watched the hanging, gleaming body, the most beautiful and terrible object he had ever seen till then. One of his father's friends reached up and in his hands he held a knife: and Jesse wished that he had been that man. It was a long, bright knife and the sun seemed to catch it, to play with it, to caress it –

> it was brighter than the fire. And a wave of laughter swept the crowd. Jesse felt his father's hands on his ankles slip and tighten. The man with the knife walked toward the crowd, smiling slightly; as though this were a signal, silence fell; he heard his mother cough. Then the man with the knife walked up to the hanging body. He turned and smiled again. Now there was silence all over the field. The hanging head looked up. It seemed fully conscious now, as though the fire had burned out terror and pain. The man with the knife took the nigger's privates in his hand. … The white hand stretched them, cradled them, caressed them. Then the dying man's eyes looked straight into Jesse's eyes – it could have been as long as a second, but it seemed longer than a year. Then Jesse screamed, and the crowd screamed as the knife flashed, first up, then down, cutting the dreadful thing away, and the blood came roaring down. Then the crowd rushed forward, tearing at the body with their hands, with knives, with rocks, with stones, howling and cursing. (Baldwin 1965: 250–1)

Recalling that memorable day when he was lifted onto the shoulders of his father to peer over the heads of the lynchers, Jesse is now old enough to lie in the darkness with his wife beside him, feeling pangs of rage and disappointment at not being able to perform sexually. He knew, of course, what he had witnessed: the screaming crowds, the torture that ensued, the castration and burning. The spectacle had left him feeling restless and excited, bewildered by 'a joy he had never felt before' (ibid.: 250). For the first time he'd understood his father's life, and couldn't help but love him. Seeing himself through the enraptured eyes of his mother and father and the doomed eyes of the black man, Jesse knows that what he has seen is a mirror in whose reflection his father had chosen to reveal 'to him a great secret which would be the key to his life forever' (ibid.: 251). Remembering that man lying 'spread-eagled with what had been a wound between what had been his legs', he knows 'that his father had carried him through a mighty test' (ibid.). Memories of that wound, still and gaping, are what allow him to enter his wife at the story's end; to 'do' her like a nigger: 'Come on, sugar, I'm going to do you like a nigger, just like a nigger, come on, sugar, and love me just like you'd love a nigger' (ibid.: 252).

Fucking his (now) nigger-loving wife, savouring the inheritance of that paternal secret, Jesse knows that what he had witnessed was a gift from his father. That gift, the desire and power to castrate – to take and so to take on – the sexuality of black men, brings them together and forges their futures as white men. Disconcertingly, what sustains Jesse (and his wife) 'as he laboured and she moaned' are the correspondences between that gift and the terrible, gaping wound (ibid.). There is much more here than simply coming. Jesse's blackface imitation of those two *scenes* – the lynching, his parents' sex which precedes it – may be sadistic, but his performance also thrives on imitating derogatory images of black men as either dangerously oversexed and/or emasculated or dead. One thing he knows for sure is this: blackness is a vicarious, disfiguring, joyful pleasure, passionately enabling as well as substitutively dead. Taught that a devotion to the love of being white can only be secured by fearing and hating black men, for white boys like Jesse, exposed to the consuming, unconscious power of such racist imagery, the costs of parting company from his father's 'lesson' was to leave oneself prone to unmanly isolation, unable to recognise oneself as a man. Furthermore, the images of black men work, as the story suggests, to contain the dread and fear of castration shaping one's frustrated desire to be *like* one's father in later life. Jesse's desire to be the man holding the knife instead of the man being cut shows a willingness to pay his dues and belong to something greater than himself, to be at one with the general will. Not being engulfed, diminished or disfigured is his reward for becoming a 'white' man. He has learned the glorious and gloriously apposite lesson that, being white, he has a privileged ownership of the phallus, whereas black men, as abject representatives of death and castration, do not.

Let's go back to that lengthy passage I've just cited: everything that I have tried to explain about lynching as spectacle in this chapter – that it is not just a form of popular theatre, or pain as public entertainment, but a ritual, cathartic act of initiation and absolution – can be seen here, albeit refined into a disconcerting view of a white southern childhood and its racialised oedipal drama. While this story is framed entirely by the hurtful, self-mutilating nature of Jesse's oedipal frustration and racist aggression, it also, in effect, registers the ongoing, unconscious power of that mutilation in the psychic lives of black men. Let's face it, if Jesse has learned to see himself through the dying man's eyes, though the shock and turmoil of seeing and hearing those enigmatic scenes and silences at night, at home, it also seems important to observe that it is Baldwin, a black gay writer, who is imagining seeing that incision – that cut – through him. Trying to untie the knots of displacement here, it occurs to me that what is striking and, at the same time, terribly depressing about *Going to Meet the Man*, is not only the spectacle of deforming – or disfiguring – black men at its centre, but Baldwin's depiction of what will be a bond of prohibition linking the black boy Otis and Jesse as future lyncher. Yet, again, this shift or transposition is all about how white and black men learn to see each other through dark, distorted mirrors; or, as Baldwin writes in 'No Name in the Street':

> And it is absolutely certain that white men, who invented the nigger's big prick, are still at the mercy of the nightmare, and are still, for the most part, doomed, in one way or another, to attempt to make this prick their own. (Baldwin 1998: 392)

'As far as personal authority went', he continues, 'one could imagine that their [white men's] shriveled faces were an exact indication of how matters were with them below the belt', and that, 'the only thing which prevented the South from being an absolutely homosexual community was, precisely, the reverberating absence of men' (ibid.: 393).

Not man enough to be homosexual or black, then, and at the mercy of a withering nightmare they are doomed to make real, white racist men cannot see beyond the black tain of the mirror. In representing white male captivation by their images of black manhood (a captivation registered in Jesse's sudden 'stiffening' after applying a cattle prod to a black man's genitals), Baldwin is also exploring, by implication, what it means for both white and black men to live their lives through the 'disagreeable mirror' of race and sex fantasies – as he puts it in his 1965 essay, 'The White Man's Guilt' (ibid.: 722). In so far as black and white men bond over those idealised desires and disdainful vilifications, a bonding which discloses their shared, but disavowed, dreams, Baldwin is also telling a general story about American culture: how it cannot see beyond its obsessions with the illusion – a favourite word – of colour; how it remains trapped by its terrible litany of projections onto black men. 'The white man's unadmitted – and apparently, to him, unspeakable – private fears and longings', Baldwin writes in his pivotal essay, 'The Fire Next Time', first published in 1963, 'are projected onto the Negro' (Baldwin 1998: 341). Those projections frame a stark, enduring legacy of how black men have been held up to the lens of American culture. That legacy, the entire point of which is to see images of black men dead but exposed, can be read alongside what Baldwin suggests, in 'The White Man's Guilt', is the strange predicament afflicting mainly white Americans; namely, they 'do not see what they see' (Baldwin 1998: 722). If white America nonetheless insists on believing what it sees to be true, rather than see its own projected anxieties and frenzied disavowals, its blindess is not primarily a white problem. As Baldwin reminds us in 'The Fire Next Time': 'All of us know', he writes, 'whether or not we are able to admit it, that mirrors can only lie, that death by drowning is all that awaits one there' (Baldwin 1998: 341). That distorted vision or double reflection, allied to an insecurity, envy and inhibitory fear of blacks, is worrisome to blacks for it can alter the whole tone of one's life. The 'Negro problem is produced by the white man's profound desire not to be judged by those who are not white, not to be seen as he is', he states, 'at the same time a vast amount of white anguish is rooted in the white man's equally profound need to be seen as he is, to be released from the tyranny of his mirror' (ibid.).

In dreams, as in life, it is difficult to avoid the scars of this double bind. These images confirm what Baldwin is trying to figure here, namely, how fantasy and trauma often act as distorted mirrors; how images and imitations can be mingled with an impulse to torture and maim. That is, again, how many whites, having barricaded themselves into a hall of inclined mirrors, enforce and perpetuate a concerted way of not seeing themselves as well as blacks. But then, if we all have learned to resemble our reflections, perhaps the best way of ensuring psychic health might be, as Baldwin observed, to appear to ourselves inverted, as in a camera obscura; shifting the horizon of our perceptions so as to celebrate and love our images *as* double reflections, no longer conceptually boxed-in by the fantasy of exact resemblances. After all, life isn't, and never has been, a self-portrait in a convex mirror nor a vanishing point beyond symptoms and dreams.

Notes

1. 'Sometimes the excised organs are rammed into the victim's mouth, to protrude like some grotesque tongue': Henry M. Miller, *The Mob's Verdict: Silence at the End of the Rope* (Chatsworth, California: Barclay House, 1974), p. 132.
2. See Jacquelyn Dowd Hall for a discussion of what she describes as the 'Southern rape complex'; or *Birth of A Nation* for a cinematic view of the 'black brute ... lurking in the dark'.
3. As Jacquelyn Dowd Hall has pointed out in her history of Jessie Daniel Ames and the Women's Campaign Against Lynching, almost 5,000 people died by lynching between 1882 and 1946. 'Until World War One', she notes, 'the average number of lynchings never fell below two or three a week' – a threat which was used to create what Richard Wright describes as a 'terrible climate of fear' for black men and women (Dowd Hall 1984: 341).

4. Compare Muhammad Ali's well-known response to seeing the battered face of Emmett Till, the black teenager murdered in Mississippi, in August 1955. His face was carried, full page and close up, in the black magazine, *Jet*, a month after the lynch-murder. 'Emmett Till and I were about the same age', Ali writes in his autobiography, *The Greatest*, in 1976:

   > A week after he was murdered. ... I stood on a corner with a gang of boys, looking at pictures of him in the black newspapers and magazines. In one, he was laughing and happy. In the other, his head was swollen and bashed in, his eyes bulging out of their sockets, and his mouth twisted and broken. ... I felt a deep kinship to him when I learned he was born the same year and day I was. I couldn't get Emmett Till out of my mind, until one evening I thought of a way to get back at white people for his death. (Ali 1976: 34)

   Identification – 'kinship': Till as Ali's 'brother' – coincides with the wish for revenge here, the desire to get back at the white people known to be responsible for the murder of Emmett Till (but not convicted by the courts when they came to trial in Mississippi in September 1955). Above all, this is a communal, or collective, looking. The images of Till were published in *black* magazines and newspapers, *for* the various black communities who, on one reading, are looking at an image of themselves – what they can become – in white culture. In other words, the dead Emmett Till was – is – an emblem of what it meant to see oneself through the eyes of white racists. 'The single story that sat atop the pinnacle of racial victimization for us was that of Emmett Till', writes Shelby Steele in 'On Being Black and Middle-Class' in 1988. 'By telling his story and others like it, we came to *feel* the immutability of our victimization, its utter indigenousness, as a thing on this earth like dirt or sand or water'. (Steele 1988: 43)
5. See also Rhoda L. Goldstein (ed.), *Black Life and Culture in the United States* (New York: Apollo, 1971), p. 242b; James H. Street, *Look Away! A Dixie Notebook* (New York: Viking, 1936), pp. 35–7; and Miller op. cit. pp. 49–56 and 121–8.

II 'Murderous Appetites': Photography and Fantasy

> My approach to photographing a flower is not much different from photographing a cock. (Robert Mapplethorpe, Interview with Gerrit Henry, 1982)

> I wanted to see what someone looked like inside. ... I like to see how things work. (Jeffrey Dahmer, cited in Masters, 1993)

> Every day the need to possess the object close-up in the form of a picture, or rather a copy becomes more imperative. (Walter Benjamin, 'A Small History of Photography', 1985)

Imagine. You're walking around 'Robert Mapplethorpe', the first major retrospective of Mapplethorpe's photography which took place at the Whitney Museum of American Art, New York, in 1989. You come across his *X Portfolio*. You stop. You look at it. What is your response? Shock? Bewilderment? Desire? Anger? Disgust? Boredom? 'Nothing in my experience or my fantasy had prepared me for an image of that sort of act, let alone a photograph that showed anything like it taking place', writes Arthur C. Danto, trying to describe his response to one of the most controversial images in Mapplethorpe's *Portfolio*: a man, clad in leather, urinating into the mouth of another man kneeling before him (Danto 1996: 7). Such images, Danto continues, are strictly outside of 'my own repertoire of fantasies': that is, Mapplethorpe's photographs come as a shock. The shock of *Richard*, for example: at first sight, Danto doesn't know what he's looking at. He looks more closely. It's a trussed-up, lacerated scrotum and penis. His first thought, Danto tells us, was that this 'had to be a photograph of some sort of sculpture'. Surely no living, 'actual person', he protests (to himself?), would undergo this willingly – this, he's forced to acknowledge, 'painful *wished-for* masochistic infliction' acted out on their bodies and person (ibid.; my italics).

Nothing in experience, or fantasy, let alone a photograph. Danto lingers before Mapplethorpe's portraits bemused, yet fascinated, by his own contemplation: 'One wanted to escape and one wanted a further contemplation' (ibid.: 10). Wanting to see more, he returns 'obsessively and repetitively', he confesses, 'to the same images and the same scenarios, over and over again' – repetition inscribing itself through the rhetoric of *Playing with the Edge* (ibid.: 7–8). The moment of looking is revelatory, unexpected: Danto is unprepared for an image which intrudes upon him, both wound and lure. What wounds, it seems, is the content of Mapplethorpe's sexual fantasies; or, more precisely, the sado-masochistic sexuality of those who people his photographs. What lures, or transfigures, Danto suggests, is the force, and form, of Mapplethorpe's artistic vision. It's a common theme in responses to Mapplethorpe. 'Startling visual poetry turns the event into a drama of aesthetics', writes Sarah Kent, in her review of the *X Portfolio* in 1996. 'Fetishism is beautifully framed; sordid acts are sanctified' (*Time Out*, 25 September 1996). Crudely, art transforms sex; Mapplethorpe sculpts with light; the moment of the aesthetic, the perfection of his artistic vision, redeems the squalid. But only if one looks again, and again: looks through the image to uncover the form, the realms of aesthetic pleasure and ascension. Gripped, and perturbed, by Mapplethorpe's photography, Danto is yet able to 'rise', through reflection, from inner havoc to inner calm. No longer excluded, violated, by the strangeness of what he sees, 'I was *exalted*', Danto concludes (ibid.: 14).

The chill, and disgust, of that first encounter has gone. Almost. On leaving the gallery, Danto has the sense of being cut and exposed, the inside of his body bared open by those unbearable, albeit beautiful, photographs. Looking at Mapplethorpe's work, he avows, was 'like undergoing surgery' (ibid.: 11, 73). Like being cut open, and having something cut in or cut out. Like being in *Richard*, perhaps; like *being* Richard, who has his penis cut in the eye of the camera. Through the act of contemplating Mapplethorpe's image, it seems, Danto takes the place of Richard, identifies with him – or with what is being done to him – by repeating the look required to transform pain into art. That identification suggests, in turn, that the sado-masochism of the image cannot be contained within the frame of the photograph. No, it passes into the relation between spectator and photograph, spectator and photographer. Danto's identification of himself as a patient 'undergoing surgery' casts Mapplethorpe as a man who cuts up bodies in the name of art (the act of laceration becoming part of the process of looking as such). Transformed from the inside out, Danto delivers his aesthetic judgement: he will take on the disturbance of Mapplethorpe's images, return to them, consume them, take them in.

Almost. Not everything in Mapplethorpe's oeuvre can be contained, or consumed, by the work of aesthetic judgement. Mapplethorpe's photographs of the black male body and, in particular, the black penis, expose Danto to another fantasmatic scene, another limit to desire in looking, but here the disgust remains. It's a scene which appears to challenge the limits of the aesthetic invested by Danto who finds himself unable to follow Mapplethorpe in his feverish judgement of the 'photographical' form of the black male body. More specifically, one of the limits to Danto's identification with Mapplethorpe's aesthetic comes in his discussion of what may be Mapplethorpe's most famous, and controversial, image of the black penis, *Man in Polyester Suit* (Fig. 2.1). '[S]ullen and heavy like the trunk of an elephant', muses Danto, reflecting on the 'folkloric' tumescence of this penis (as if, like an elephant's trunk, it can feed the black man's mouth). Hanging, 'veiny and pulpy', on the outside of the black man's suit, his penis is, to push the point, on the outside of the civilised. '[H]is penises are so exotically weird', writes Andrew Graham-Dixon in response to the same photograph, 'they seem inhuman, like some parasite species that has managed to graft itself on to the human form. ... The penis looks like an elephant's trunk, not really human at all – certainly not civilised' (*Independent*, 21 September 1996). (Remember Skinny Slaton: Don't look human, does it?) It is, I think, striking that neither Danto nor Graham-Dixon says that what they are looking at is a black penis, though both find themselves talking in terms of the non-human: the black penis as bestial, elephantine. A type of displacement at the level of rhetoric, perhaps, one that puts the black penis on the outside of both the civic and the aesthetic. In Danto's words, *Man in Polyester Suit* 'puts the viewer on edge by aestheticizing the photograph while leaving the penis the difficult and dangerous thing it is' (Danto 1996: 111). 'The photograph may be beautiful', he continues, 'without the penis rendered in it becoming derivatively beautiful': in other words, Mapplethorpe cannot transfer his aesthetic vision to this thing which has to remain, Danto tells us, 'incompletely aestheticized', 'unredeemed' and 'shocking' (ibid.: 106, 111).

Not something you'd want to take in, then, via eye or mouth. Danto remains in the unaestheticised realm of disgust. But what if looking is a form of incorporation, of taking something inside (this may be part of its anxiety?). Let's note that judgement, for Freud

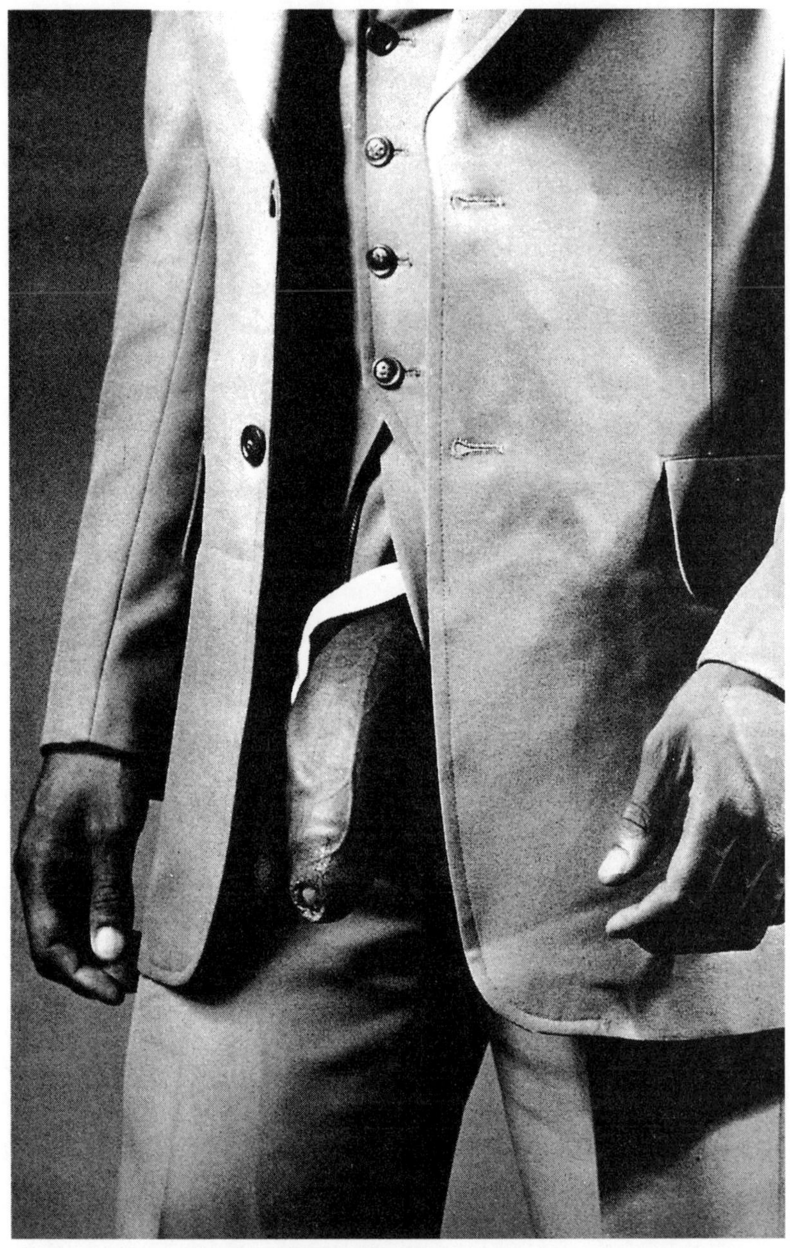

2.1 Robert Mapplethorpe, *Man in Polyester Suit* (1980) from *The Black Book* (1986). Copyright © 1980 The Estate of Robert Mapplethorpe.

(and in our context, this is telling), is always a question of taking something into the mouth or spitting it out. An insight that the German psychoanalyst, Otto Fenichel, will develop in terms of incorporation, or devoration, by the eyes. 'When someone gazes intensely at an object', writes Fenichel at the beginning of his 'The scopophilic instinct and identification', first published in 1935, 'we say that he "devours it with his eyes," and there are many similar phrases' (Fenichel 1935: 373). The symbolic equation to look at = to devour, supports Fenichel's remarkable extension of Freud's theory of scopophilia: the drive to look at a sexual object. 'The eye', Fenichel writes, 'is conceived of as an organ that robs and bites' (ibid.: 395). It can even, in fantasy, give access to the interior of the body. Wanting to devour, to take something in via the eyes, can run parallel, in Fenichel's view, with the wish to destroy something by looking at it; 'or else', he writes, 'the act of looking itself has already acquired the significance of a modified form of destruction' (ibid.: 377). Fenichel's conventional, but telling, example of such a destructive way of looking is the woman who expresses her wish to castrate the man by looking in the region of his genitals. That is, to look at the penis and to castrate, and destroy it, can amount to the same thing (ibid.).[1]

To incorporate, to eat, through the eyes; to want to look, and look again, in the name of appreciating and destroying, loving and hating. How do you start to tell the difference between the two? What is Fenichel describing if not the psychical processes which can support, and derange, the act of looking – and, in particular, the act of looking at photographs? 'Let me remind you', Fenichel concludes, 'that man's mechanical ingenuity has actually created a "devouring eye", which looks at and incorporates the external world and later projects it outward again. I refer, of course, to the camera' (ibid.: 395). On both sides of the images then: if the camera is a devouring eye, one that robs and bites and cuts into people, the photograph is a product of that movement of introjection and projection, an object through which to trace the movement of devouring and spitting out.

For Danto, the penis in *Man in Polyester Suit* is ugly, pulpy, bestial: it turns hunger into nausea, art into disgust. It becomes a thing, immoveable; unlike those images of coprophagia and genital laceration in *X Portfolio*, *Man in Polyester Suit* can only ever be found wanting, spat out. Inedible, the black penis cannot be judged or aesthetically valued, taken in and savoured. A sight to be kept outside but, and crucially, the image is also trying to force its way in: after all, unless we close our eyes, we cannot help but register what we see. Walking around 'Robert Mapplethorpe', the spectator is looking at what

Mapplethorpe wants him, or her, to see (what Mapplethorpe has *made happen*). 'I wanted people to see that even those extremes could be made into art', Mapplethorpe insisted in 1988. 'Take those pornographic images and make them somehow transcend the image' (Mapplethorpe, cited in Celant 1992: 38). The risk of looking at whatever a photographer like Mapplethorpe chooses to exhibit, then, is that you might see something you don't want to see; quite simply, you might be shocked, and he might fail to engage you in his aesthetic, even though you're prepared to look, and look again. The question is where does such (obsessive) looking leave you? What defence do you have against the disgust generated by an image made irredeemable by lack or excess? Against a failure in identification with, or aestheticisation of, a photograph? The type of defence described by Fenichel, perhaps: a devouring scopophilia. Take it in so that you can control it, torment it, spit it out. But the image will leave its trace.

Mapplethorpe's images can threaten and disgust; they can also treat you as a phobic object. At least, that was a key element of Kobena Mercer's challenging interpretation of Mapplethorpe's photography in 'Imaging the Black Man's Sex', first published in 1986. Mercer has made his own repeated returns to Mapplethorpe's photographs, testimony to the disturbance that these images can unleash. As a black, gay critic, Mercer was able to find himself both inside and outside the frame of Mapplethorpe's images, implicated in a range of fantasmatic scenarios at once homoerotic and racist. There is an aggression in Mapplethorpe's aesthetic, Mercer argues in 1986, and it starts to show up an aggression in the act of looking as such. 'The camera cuts away', he writes (the terms recall Danto), 'like a knife, allowing the spectator to inspect the "goods"' (Mercer 1994: 183). Again, Mapplethorpe is cutting up, cutting away at, a black male body; his 'black fever', in Mercer's view, a response to the frustration aroused by his own fetishistic investment in that 'forbidden totem of colonial fantasy': the black phallus (ibid.). Frustration because, seducing his spectators into fascination with the surface and sculpture of black skin – this is the fetishistic structure of the photographs which reduces black men to 'homogeneous type[s] thoroughly saturated with a totality of sexual predicates' – Mapplethorpe both affirms and denies the myth of the potent, sometimes monstrous, black penis (ibid.: 174).

Affirms and denies: by 1989, that ambivalence has come right to the fore of Mercer's reading of Mapplethorpe. Writing intimately, revealingly, in 'Skin Head Sex Thing: Racial Difference and the Homoerotic Imaginary', Mercer describes his own feelings of emotional ambivalence and bemoans the 'residual moralism' of earlier readings, including his own, of Mapplethorpe's racial fetishism (Mercer 1994: 190). Fetishism, Mercer suggests, is not necessarily 'a bad thing' (ibid.). (Though we might want to linger on the question of whether or not racial fetishism can be a *good* thing?) No longer angry, but turned on. Mercer's two essays reveal a fissure (in the images, in himself) which runs from his angry clamour over how the black models are viewed to a shared, homoerotic desire to look. In 1986, it is as if Mercer can only see himself *in* the frame ('my angry emphasis on racial fetishism as a potentially exploitative process of objectification was based on the way in which I felt identified with the black men in the field of vision simply by virtue of sharing the same "categorical" identity as a black man' (ibid.: 193)); by 1989, he is on the other side of the camera, acknowledging the homosexual desire to look ('Thus, sharing the same desire to look, I am forced to confront the rather unwelcome fact that I would actually occupy the same position in the fantasy of mastery that I said was that of the white male subject' (ibid.: 193)). In short, Mercer is sliding between anger and desire, being black and being gay, objectification and fantasy. It is as if he wants to devour what he sees while being the object of himself looking. At the same time, the anxiety, the paranoia internal to that looking is, for Mercer, inseparable from the scene of looking itself. Routing his way tenaciously, choosing to confront his divided identifications, Mercer retraces his steps to arrive at the following conclusion: 'the visual image objectified an object-choice that was already there in my fantasies and wishes' (ibid.: 193). While, in his earlier line of argument, Mercer could see no difference between the eye of Mapplethorpe's camera and a racist vision of black men, he now finds a genuine equivocity agitating through his – Mapplethorpe's – photography. 'The difficult and troublesome question raised by Mapplethorpe's black male nudes', Mercer acknowledges against himself, '– do they reinforce or undermine racist myths about black sexuality? – is strictly unanswerable, since his aesthetic strategy makes an unequivocal yes/no response impossible' (ibid.: 192).

Having saved fetishism, then, Mercer is able to save Mapplethorpe's 'perverse aestheticism': the cutting and slicing that, a few years before, generates the rhetoric of a black body as slave-commodity, goods to be inspected and sold. Now 'the image throws the question back to the spectator', Mercer suggests, 'for whom its undecidability is experienced precisely as the unsettling shock effect' (ibid.: 192). In other words, aesthetic shock is a question which cannot be answered, a question that cannot be thrown back to the image. Or, it seems, to Mapplethorpe who, as a white photographer – rather than as, say, a gay one – falls outside the frame of Mercer's reading at this point. Certainly, Mercer's revision, and complication, of his previously angry response to Mapplethorpe moves his argument forward; but, and crucially, he now remains more or less silent on the racial, or negrophobic, aspects of Mapplethorpe's work. Admitting that his anger was prompted by envy of, and rivalry with, Mapplethorpe – a white man who had access to those beautiful black bodies – Mercer, it turns out, acted as if someone had broken in and stolen his repertoire of fantasies (ibid.: 194). Painfully reminiscent of Freud's account of the young male fetishist, Mercer suggests that he could not endure wanting to look at Mapplethorpe's photographs for fear that he wouldn't like what he saw; or, as he puts it in 1986, in an essay co-authored with Isaac Julien: '*we want to look, but do not always find the images we want to see*' (ibid.: 133). After all, you might not want to see what Mapplethorpe wants you to look at. A shared desire to look may not be the same as a shared way of looking.

I want to throw that question back to Mapplethorpe's aestheticism, to understand how scopophilia and negrophobia come together in his work (a question central to the tensions between Mercer's two readings). We can start to glimpse that articulation by reading across two photographs which appear back to back in *The Black Book* (1986): *Hooded Man* and *Man in Polyester Suit*. *Hooded Man*, for example, forces us to confront, with something like ferocious irony, a history of looking at black men in lynching scenes and images (Fig. 2.2). Apparently courting the accusation of racial sadism towards the black male body, Mapplethorpe imposes those scenes and images on his hooded model (the same model featured in *Man in Polyester Suit*), as the iconography of the Ku Klux Klan stares out at us from the frame. To look, as a black male spectator, at such an image is to be aware of a leash around your neck, one formed by racial fear and sadistic fantasy and the terrifying-satisfying spectacle of castration. Treat the photo as a mirror (as a point of identification), and you find your face is missing, displaced by a heavily loaded racial icon or figurehead. Watching that pose, seeing how it connects to a history of drawn-out abasement, other scenes appear inside the frame. Put yourself in the pose and those circling arms become a noose. They embrace the imaginary weight of a racist icon; they expose your masochistic desire. The missing caption should read: 'I cannot resist what is no longer hidden'. *Hooded Man* is thus a study of compressed time, of victims and witnesses, but it is not documentary. It is practically rubbing our faces in an uncomfortable

2.2 Robert Mapplethorpe, *Hooded Man* (1980) from *The Black Book* (1986). Copyright © 1980 The Estate of Robert Mapplethorpe.

scene of black desolation. Or, is it? Perhaps the image is a call to appropriation? A call to the black man to take on (to imitate?) the mask of racist aggression, to send it back from whence it came.

These questions recall Mercer's divided response to *Man in Polyester Suit*, his wish to make this image answerable to the look it solicits as he comes to occupy the place of Mapplethorpe's devouring eye. Yet this very kind of appetite for the image – the same kind of appetite we saw uncovered in the previous chapter when the imago of black sexuality is destroyed – forces Mercer to see himself from the same position as that of racial scopophilia. Remember Claude Neal, forced to consume his own penis as part of a racist spectacle through which the white spectators (in Fenichel's terms) devour him via their eyes – devour his devouring, savouring the deathly pleasure on his lips. Think back to the scenes of looking and tearing, mutilating and photographing black men, which are the history of lynching in the United States (scenes preserved, of course, on camera). Wanting to look, then, but not liking what he sees, the troubling coincidence between Mercer's looking and Mapplethorpe's look suggests that self-devoration is one way of incorporating the shock of these images. Again, if looking at and castrating, destroying, the black penis, can amount to the same thing, how do you tell the difference between wanting to be looked at as if you were inside the image, and looking at yourself consuming the image? To put this slightly differently, Mapplethorpe's photography exposes the way that a scopophilic kind of looking cannot be contained within the photograph, an exposure which puts enormous pressure on Mercer's ability to tell the difference between representation and spectatorship and the racial scopophilia that links them: crudely, inside or outside the frame? Do these images cleanse us, black men, of our inhibitions only by allowing us to feed well off our own abjection? While my answer is yes yes, those yeses are far from straightforward, for they relay between an identification of what is bearable and the collusive (perhaps perverse) fantasy of having something too secret, even, to be consumed or spat out. Far from taking us outside of ourselves, Mapplethorpe's photographs drive us dimly inward, allowing us to see things otherwise unperceived. They cause an ungovernable tremor inside us, one which cuts through both history and logic. They also refuse any easy condemnation or anger by forcing us to consider how and why sadistic forms of looking cannot help but devour their subjects – a forced awareness that in no way prevents such annihilation from taking place.

This problem remains central to Mercer's 1986 reading of *Man in*

Polyester Suit and his account of Mapplethorpe's reduction of the black man to the black penis. According to Mercer, this image reduces, or condenses, the black male body to the penis: '*apart from his hands*', he writes, 'it is the penis and the penis alone that identifies the model in the photograph as a black man' (ibid.: 174, my italics). Apart from his hands, the myth of the 'big black willy' is there, hung and framed, available for everyone to see (ibid.: 191). That myth, he continues, represents a typing of black men (a type which, I would add, Mapplethorpe privately referred to as his 'Super Nigger' (Mapplethorpe, cited in Morrisroe 1995: 234)). But why part the penis from those neatly poised hands? Or, to put the question in a different way, why frame the penis with those hands, their slightly open fingers, promising to touch its hung, slightly erect unfolding? By excluding those hands from his interpretation of *Man in Polyester Suit*, Mercer risks the same reductive (and fetishistic) vision of which he accuses Mapplethorpe. Without those hands we lose sight of, overlook even, the scopophilic work of the photograph, which teasingly offers, as it undermines and sets apart, the relation between the threat of the black man's sex and the veneer of civilisation. The poise of those hands which, with the semi-erect penis, form a triptych – hanging relaxed, and unceremonious, at the model's sides – marks the frame with a certain question. What are they going to *do*? Poised, as if for movement – in this, *Man in Polyester Suit* is not quite a 'still' life – they suggest an erotic mobility and plasticity sometimes missing from Mapplethorpe's black nude poses. After all, what do hands do? They press, hold, touch, stroke, squeeze, hit and strangle. They are hardly ever passive things. The polyester suit also forms an edge, a border, between the hands and penis, between black and white: in Mapplethorpe's view, only a nigger would wear that suit (Mapplethorpe cited ibid.: 248). Forming an inverted 'v' above the model's exposed penis, the trousers are stretched because ill-fitting; the organ simply hangs there, waiting to edge out under the weight of its own heat, to be fondled and caressed. There is the fiercest kind of concentrated stillness in the overall composition, and one which threatens to implode just beneath the surface of the cloth, an implosion which may be part of the sadistic promise of the picture. That is, the penis and hands have been arranged – posed – so that we might see, take a closer look at, the source of what underpins much racist pornography.

For those who have seen this picture up-close, *Man in Polyester Suit* is remarkably flat (even for a photograph). Although tiny rents of light and shadow open up in places, the entire effect is drab and monochrome, a vision foreclosed just for the thrill of it. Hidden in partial dark, the shaft of the penis also emerges out of a combination of light and darkness, as if its nakedness had been pressed into an almost sculptural pose enabling us to study its length and its tip. There is nothing casual about this pose. Its force lies in what we bring to it: a history that refuses to fade with memory, a way of seeing black male sexuality that not only unsettles, but is marked by a withdrawal of black men from any vestiges of the civilised, the human. A way of seeing demanding the direct, memorial confirmation of the camera. Into this unrelenting, and disfiguring, imaging, Mapplethorpe's black male nudes act as complicit reflections, rather than deconstructions, of the racial scopophilia driving their working.

Once again, it is a question of who is looking and who is being looked at, a question which has always been central to the violence enacted by whites against black men. In what may appear to be an outrageous association, I want now to consider another, and more infamous, instance of racial scopophilia in which the work of the camera comes right to the fore: the image-corpus of the serial killer, Jeffrey Dahmer. As photographer, and cannibal, Dahmer appears to embody – at the limits of both psyche and culture – Fenichel's understanding of the camera as a type of devouring eye. In this sense, I want to suggest, he allows us another glimpse into the strange, and ruthless, world of wanting to look at black men.

Not all stories are reparable. Here is one told postmortem. It begins with the photographs of an 'autopsy' randomly arranged in the top drawer of a chest.

Nearly all the victims are black or Asian men. None of the photographs is dated nor arranged in any chronological order. None is captioned and the names of the victims are missing. Their very randomness attests to some unknowable code or key. It signifies a secret connection, a series of vague snapshots whose meaning and story has long since disappeared along with the person who took them. They frame, and focus, a ferocious contact, becoming a type of visual diary that maps bodies naked and abed, ripped open and dismembered, innards exposed, eyes staring out at the camera from decapitated heads. These photographs are voyeuristic and repetitive, professional and exhibitionist. A stash of private pornography complicit with some deeply sequestered need, some irresistibly exquisite and memorial pleasure. Some of the bodies are arranged in the simulation of a peaceful, perhaps loving, sleep, taken with infinite care. Others show bodies grappling and straining, in the throes of an unimaginable pain and panic. An incorporation even a cannibal would have to spit out. They are arresting and shocking, desperate and pitiful. These photographs once belonged to the serial killer, Jeffrey Dahmer. They are now in the possession of the State of Wisconsin, carefully preserved under lock and key.

When one of the arresting officers, Rolf Mueller, first discovered these photographs in a chest of drawers in Dahmer's bedroom at 924 North 25th Street, his first thought was that they were simulations, or fakes. As if such indignities could only be inflicted on sculptures or models (on men no longer living?); as if only an 'artificial' camera eye could record such horrendous acts. The idea that the bodies could have been made to appear unreal did not occur to Mueller. Nor did he suspect that these bodies, now lifeless, were made to adopt a singular pose. The race of these men did not register at first, only their body-parts. (This oversight will go unwritten in the records.) After the first shock, Mueller grabbed a handful of snaps and returned to the living room where his partner, Robert Rauth, was holding Dahmer, restrained and handcuffed on the floor. 'These are real pictures', Mueller reportedly told him (cited in Masters 1993: 3).

As real pictures these photographs allowed Dahmer to get up real close, eyeball tight, to visualise and manifest a desire, an extreme *coup de force*, that, in dismembering its objects, collapsed or blurred what, in fantasy, they supposedly were a counterfeit or copy of – something unreadable or non-narratable in the actual image (or photograph), something uncanny and unforeseen.

These photographs reveal the details of a life reputedly absorbed by the slow, convulsive, interior rhythms of black male torsos and bodies. Dahmer's addiction to black 'meat' was not drawn by heat or by smell, but by sinew and bone. He turned abdomens and thighs into mirrors and lures; faces and muscles into compulsion and ritual; unbreathable confessions of love into blessings for a journey beyond any moral law. His abiding interest in the corporeal was also matched by a desire to see and to devour, to keep an image of an attractive body. He wanted to preserve the looks of the men he desired, to make them 'a permanent part of me'; to 'completely control a person, a person that I found physically attractive, and keep them with me as long as possible, even if it meant just keeping a part of them' (Dahmer cited in Hirsch 1996: 447, 446). A post-mortem pornography, maybe, one that uses the glossy veneer of the photograph as the media through which the elusive human murmur of his victims can be relived, transformed into the treasured memory of his private and personal loves. But was the best way of killing them to take their pictures; or the best way of picturing them to see them dead? And were these images fantasy enhancements or real reinstitutions of how he saw himself reflected in them; a true copy of an image eaten and inside him, or prophylactic signs of an irredeemable loss? Dahmer took pictures of his victims because he could possess them only when they were dead. Dead they offered no resistance to his image of them. Dead they became floating zones of desire exactly equivalent to their ideal penetrability. At such moments, he could sever and recombine them at will, he could even 'fix' them up with someone else. He could change their preferred attachments, slice by slice, altering the life as originally lived. Only by posthumously possessing – eating – his victims could he account for and so narrate how he had been absolutely possessed by them. He was their medium of release while simultaneously catering to his own manufactured love.

These photographs depict bodies in ruins, sliced open to the cruel yet determined gaze of a man known to be obsessed by medical pathology and typology. Dahmer honed his photographic technique in the military, a year after murdering and dissecting his first victim. Training as a medical specialist, '[h]e learned the fine points of human anatomy through diagrams, schematics and vivid photography' (cited in Seltzer 1998: 192). As 'types', his victims were subjected to hours of insatiable, analytic scrutiny. Indexed and lovingly pared down to a denotative shorthand, they were wondered over and worked at, sculpted and shaped, codified and exposed by his camera. Treating his victims as sites of revelation made accessible through repeated acts of surgical mutilation, the heightened clarity of a photograph allowed him to continue his studies long after his physiognomic specimens had become unuseable. Skins and body parts, in other words, were invested with affects that required the elevation and distancing, and the cutting eye of the camera.

While this bizarre 'enshrinement and desecration' also marks the aura of photographic memorabilia at lynching scenes, Mark Seltzer, in his compelling *Serial Killers*, uses the word 'taxidermic' to describe this drive to image – to capture – that strangely anonymous economy of promises and debts linking victim and serial killer (ibid.: 55). Dahmer's use of the camera to typify and reduce his victims also borders on what I would want to call the 'photodermic'. Knowing that a reek and staleness, and a certain impurity, would eventually come to destroy his possessions, Dahmer turned to photography to remove – to sublimate – that threat. Photography allowed him to retard signs of decay and decomposition by converting his subjects' lives into still lifes, dead fantasies, etched and fixed on his retina. Here the photograph, by cutting loose from its malodorous origin, effectively isolated and arrested Dahmer's dreams of infinitely repeatable – infinitely readable – accessibility to his victims' interiors, albeit through the detour of representation. Whether they were buried in a pool of soilex, or effaced by a film of emulsion, he took satisfaction in the detailed, ordinarily unseen, insides of bodies, images that seemed to reveal a shadowy world of rarely spied metamorphosis, a space or gap where life and interiority no longer coincided. Even if those photographic images launched desire beyond what they permitted him to see – off-frame – they nonetheless provided him with the consolation of lives endlessly unmade and reimagined, mimetically frozen and preserved against transformation and loss. By printing these images of scattered remains – lungs, intestines, penises, livers and hearts – Dahmer effectively devoured his victims by converting them into reusable signs and representations. These 'sitters' – denuded of consciousness and life, sacrificially and violently compelled to give up their natural appearances – workwise would always be perfectly still.

By taking photographs, in other words, even if they no longer referred to the lives from which they were taken, Dahmer could close his eyes, safe in the knowledge that, at any time, he could take possession of his keepsakes and relive what he had voraciously subtracted from them via a shared *mise-en-scène*, a bitter-sweet taste in the mouth. Sometimes the rigours of his camera work were so intense he became literally stiff with the desire to enter the spectacle he'd created, to coincide with and embrace the remains of his 'lovers'. What he saw as he cut and edited, peered and masturbated into the enclosedness, the darkness of those interiors, was a deeply unfamiliar but strangely revelatory sight. Dahmer had, in fact, created his own unique *camera obscura* on whose veiny, visceral backdrop he'd witnessed some deeper meaning or knowledge literally incarnated – embodied – through the corporeal media of black men. Incorporating all his desires and disappointments, his lost hopes and loves, that *camera obscura* had literally given body to his deepest, necrophilic fantasies. According to the journalist, Brian Masters, in *The Shrine of Jeffrey Dahmer*, his 1993 account of the criminal case, photography allowed Dahmer to 'turn life and death into a graspable object – in fact draining them of any meaning beyond the necrophilic fantasy' (Masters 1993: 146).[2] If such images answer what, in psychic terms, could be called an erotics of laceration buried deep inside him, for Dahmer, the consolation of such an image – dead but intact – lay in knowing that even though the lacerated body is not his its image satisfies his longing that it become a part of him. That knowledge, passing telepathically – corporeally – between Dahmer and his subjects, envelops these intimate portrait studies, transforming their metonymic significance into symbolic metaphors of an all-consuming love and a perishable, tactile beauty. From them he took solace that, despite being cut from their living, threatening presences, his lovers would always remain buried inside him.

And what of those men and boys picked up at clubs and malls, seduced by the financial lure of having their pictures taken at Dahmer's apartment? After the initial disquiet of being looked at – contracted – by a stranger, we do not know what finally persuaded them to agree to perform, to act-out, his wish that they pose before his camera lens to have their portraits taken. Did they feel specially favoured in being singled out in this way, by a white man bearing the promise of love and money for some easy work? A man whom some of them are reported to have found attractive? It is hard to avoid the racial elements of the story here. Black men tend to be unseen except as threats. They are mostly poor and invisible, humanly invisible to many whites who see a type entirely alien and extraneous to them, a generic emblem at best, undesirable and dangerous. This nullification gives birth to a dependable solitude, a learning to be unseen, unloved. Into this bracing form of self-awareness walks a man who, though essentially artless, clearly has a fervent appetite to consume – to look at and to own – their images, to share a certain specular intimacy and pleasure. A photographer keen to exploit and capture their desirable likenesses, if only they would consent. Either way, they were invited and engaged with, intrigued by Dahmer's whiteness and his money, encouraged by their own moral masochism. In his approach to them, cherishing their looks and bodies, little did they know that he was already visualising the scene of disfiguring penetration, a time when his black lovers, drugged and asleep – or no longer breathing – were to be violated, shorn of their forms and likenesses, refigured in an admixture of photodermic emulation and destructive love.

All the black men he murdered went someway into his mouth – a sort of ruinous conversation, a way of interring and savouring something meaningful and worshipped, enveloped and dead. Filled with their visceral presences, their accents and their smells, nothing of his victims – in fantasy – went wasted or unseen. Buried deep inside him – dead but breathing, living because dead – his victims were kept secret, deposited, to be swallowed and exhumed again and again. In this final inpouring of love, their lifeless parts wordlessly ingested and consumed, his victims were forced to eternally renew their promise to stay and not to go. Photography may be a carnal media, allowing him to conserve himself against the loss of his subjects, but here the act of inviting the dead (the no longer absent one) to come inside his mouth literally exceeds both metaphor and representation. Unlike photography, which 'didn't satisfy whatever craving I had', eating the dead for Dahmer, far from making him feel ashamed or forlorn, made him feel oddly and humanly loved and alive (Dahmer, cited in Masters 1993: 161). By putting these men inside his mouth he made them answerable – accountable – to the awesome anger and idealisation that fed him. Using his tongue to taste the corpses concealed in his mouth, taking a bite and swallowing his own indigestible love, Dahmer transformed eating into the last rites of a delicious, though lonely, burial. Tonguing the dead he could re-disfigure, re-devour them in ways that bound their images to the inside of his body. Wedging them from inside his teeth he could lick and savour them without losing them to the nostalgic – memorial – time of the photograph. As though photography was singularly inadequate as a substitute for necrophagia, unable to fill the void – that gap – in his psyche. And as though his necrophagia could take place in the absence of the deathly preservation of the photograph.[3]

Having eaten and magically worked through the effects of that separation, that verdict, the deeply discoloured and inconsumable remains of his victims were either flushed down the toilet or put out with the garbage. Although disturbing, there is a simple and stunning referentiality here, at once allegorical and tautological: black men may be eaten and excreted because, visually speaking, they already resemble shit. Their opened bodies and smells marked a shameful boundary, for Dahmer, between his homophobia and his racism, his mouth and his anus. Heard constantly muttering about 'niggers' at the Ambrosia chocolate factory where he worked, feeling guilty and trapped by his sexual fantasies and desires, Dahmer was driven to literally eat his poison, to lay waste to waste. If black gay men desired shit – so the racist homophobia ran – he would match their appetites by turning them back into shit, the shit from which they began. Dahmer thus used their polluted and irresistibly contaminating bodies to bequeath the act and signature of his own paradoxical self-mirroring. That impassable boundary between black rectums and his white mouth, that insatiable desire to have death in the mouth, to eat shit, consequently revealed a more profound guilt.

As the *sign of a polluting infection*, black men can be ripped open and consumed – that is, framed by the eye, taken into the mouth –

because, in essence, they represent the place where the shame and nausea produced by excreta becomes visible. As reeking tombs in the public life of culture, black men can be cannibalised, shredded and torn open because, like the living dead, they are imagined as vicious and parasitic, insatiably feeding off the lives of their living, white hosts. And as invasive figures in the anxious dreams of American culture, they are glimpsed as some viciously empty, ravening thing. We may never know what loomed into Dahmer's line of vision when he saw a potential victim, what war raged in his eyes when he saw those meaty, black apparitions arrayed before him. Was it a necrophilic mirror reflecting his own suppressed desires for a lifeless, perfectly still, world? Was it a mechanical mass of bone and tissue, free of any human presence, automated and overfed, without volition? Perhaps only a part of this is true. Dahmer's fierce hunger for eyes always open, never closed – a pleasure hidden away in prints stacked away in the top drawer of a chest – gave him access (albeit in photodermic form) to a post-mortem *camera obscura*, all the eye was meant for. These pictures bear witness to a demand to make black men absent from the scene of the human, while lining the eye with deep, libidinal satisfaction. That separation, delicately and carefully done, has a history in American culture as clear as daylight. If the pictures Dahmer wakened to allowed him to sleep deeply and long, that was because the person who had just died was, being black, already carrying the visible warning signs and burial markers of American culture: a black disinterred remnant visible (as the camera flashes on and off) on the proud edges of a wound. This disinterring – in fantasy – of black male bodies from any sense of personhood, is necessarily affiliated with a cultural obsession with black male sexuality as a *jouissance* incapable of any self-restraint or ascesis. Dahmer chose black men because he could capture their images without surcease, grabbing their pricks and their bodies if need be for his own disposal. What matter if they came in his eye or his mouth, his ecstasy lay in his eyesight, as ravenous in appetite as his mouth. As though, rather than images, he wanted to feed, and feed well, on something he delimited as beyond the edges of perception, something defiled and unredeemed, carnal and virile, abject and socially dead.

Through this chapter I've been arguing that the camera has played a key role in defining how black men are seen. Distorted and fantasmatic images of white desire, black men have been obliged to take part in a fatal scenario, consumed by what James Cameron calls the 'murderous appetite' of racist culture (Cameron 1995: 61). In this fable, our dreamwork is an eye fixed by someone else's fascinations and repulsions, a distorting emanation sent to possess, to consume us. No amount of irony can ever erase the historical trace – on the borderline of the frame – of the rage accompanying this exhibition, nor the savage violence at the edges of its close-up. The history of that looking, it might be argued, reveals a trait of wanting to devour, to destroy and modify via the eyes. To incorporate, to eat, through the eyes is, in Fenichel's terms, the product of the devouring eye of the camera. These are appetites that *disfigure* us, indistinguishable from a gaping wound in our fantasies and dreams – those mainstays of our imaginary lives. In the next chapter, I want to explore how black men have responded to these predominantly violent social ties, along with the persistent demand that they perform the role of fulfilling someone else's nightmare. By inverting the image, perhaps, as Alexander Crummell attempts to do through his incisive thinking on the connections among blackness, manhood and nationality. Crummell credits black men with a higher, more prescient sight, in whose anthropological essence, or type, lies the ability to devour all the forms, images and likenesses of others. In Crummell's vision of the black eye as a paradigmatic, or primal devourer, there is an identification between blackness and imitation that produces an entirely different movement of introjection and projection than racial scopophilia. A movement that will problematise racial difference as such.

Notes

1. Fenichel's development of Freud's concept of scopophilia is itself worked through the case history in which the fantasy of being raped by a negro plays a central part. The association between wanting to see, wanting to incorporate, and the fear of being torn apart by the father's penis – a fear projected here, as elsewhere in the psychoanalytic literature, on the rapacious black man – runs through Fenichel's analysis of this case. How this rape fantasy influences Fenichel's theory of vision and drive I hope to take up elsewhere.
2. Masters also associates necrophilia with a drive against life, as if loving the dead somehow amounted to hating their opposite. That opposition allows him to construe Dahmer's use of photography as further evidence of his perversion, rather than pursue the deeper resonances between Dahmer's scopophilia, photography and death.
3. For the analysts, Nicholas Abraham and Maria Torok, it is important to distinguish between the psychic process known as introjection – the casting inside – from the fantasy of incorporation, which they

distinguish 'as we would distinguish between metaphoric and photographic images' (*The Shell and the Kernel*, Vol. 1. Ed., trans. Nicholas Rand, 1994, Chicago and London: University of Chicago Press, p. 127). The figurative lure of metaphor is, for them, linked to reality and language, whereas necrophagy and coprophagy are presented as examples of '*anti-incorporation*' and '*antimetaphor*' (ibid.: 130, 132).

III Black Types

Type a. *Theol.* To prefigure or foreshadow as a type; to represent in prophetic similitude. b. = TYPIFY. (*Oxford English Dictionary*)

'We say to every colored man, *be a man where you are*': so writes the black abolitionist, Frederick Douglass, in February 1852, advising the readers of his *Frederick Douglass Paper* to 'be a man here' – here, now, in America. 'If you can't do that here', he continues, 'you can't do it there' (Douglass 1950: 173). Challenging, even reproachful, Douglass's address to the 'educated men' of black America was intended to come down on the side of the struggle for abolition (the liberation of black men and women from slavery and granting of full civic and political rights) and against the 'emigrationists' or 'colonizationists': those who, as Edward Blyden was to put it in a visit to America in 1862, were of the opinion that 'the Negro can never attain in this country to the distinction of true manhood' (Blyden 1971: 12). 'The truth is, dear Madame', Douglass writes to Harriet Beecher Stowe in March 1853, reiterating his theme of nationality and manhood, 'we are *here*, and here we are likely to remain. Individuals emigrate – nations never' (Douglass 1950: 229).

Individuals emigrate – nations never: one of the individuals, men, with whom Douglass is taking issue in the early 1850s is the black intellectual, Alexander Crummell. A less familiar figure than Douglass, perhaps, Crummell was one of the founding voices of black nationalism, an Episcopalian missionary whose complicated allegiance to the cause of racial uplift – in America and, notably, Liberia – was to produce one of the most sustained, and problematic, reflections on the connections among race, nation and manhood: the destiny of the black race as a nation, the destiny of black men as leaders of that nation. Central to that problematic, and to the dissent between Douglass and Crummell, is the idea of type: black types, male types, prototypes, typecast; black men as figures, or symbols, *of* something else: lust, violence, sexuality, degeneracy or, for thinkers of black nationalism, the ideal and exemplar of civic manliness; black men as icons and models (both Douglass and Crummell, in different ways, are asked to be *representative* of their race, to set themselves up as leaders by example); black men as image and imitation, the 'type' that imitates: 'The Negro, with a mobile and plastic nature', Crummell will argue, in 1877, 'with a strong receptive faculty, seizes upon and makes over to himself, by imitation, the better qualities of others' (Crummell 1995: 50). The idea of type – everywhere, but, at the same time, curiously unthought – belongs to this typical thinking of black character, the nature of black men, in its relation to nation, race and destiny.

Both in pursuit of, struggling for, the future of Afro-Americans, Douglass and Crummell leave us – black men, black cultural critics – with the legacy of type. What does it mean to be, or be seen to be, a 'type'? Can the idea of type be used to question the process of being typecast, stereotyped? Can we broach the topic of black national leadership in mid to late nineteenth-century America without thinking through the history of types: the ideals, and the fictions, with which, and against which, men like Douglass and Crummell were fighting? How did they respond to themselves, and each other, as image, idol and icon? Did they think of themselves, and each other, as conforming to type? And, more pressing for me, what type, or types, of black man do these thinkers traffic through their various political writings and campaigns?

Because his writing, and politics, is driven by a discourse of the black man as symbol, type, imitator – as a typological sign of the future of the black nation – the writings of Alexander Crummell will be central to this chapter. Edward Blyden's contrasting accounts of black men as icons, types and antitypes of nationality, will also be discussed for the light they cast on Crummell's ideas of race and imitation.

For Douglass, as we've just seen, Crummell's decision to emigrate to Liberia in May 1853 is characteristic of the educated black man. 'It would seem that education and emigration go together with us', he continues – wistfully, angrily – in his letter to Harriet Beecher Stowe, 'for as soon as a man rises amongst us, capable, by his genius and learning, to do us a great service, just so soon he finds that he can serve himself better by going elsewhere' (Douglass 1950: 231). It should be said that, given his earlier, public opposition to colonisation, Crummell's decision to emigrate took many by surprise especially those, the Abolitionists, who had contributed funds to his education in England (at Cambridge) between 1849 and 1853.

Further, for many Afro-Americans, including Crummell's own father, apologists for colonisation were suspected of being irredeemably racist in their campaign to transfer America's freedman population somewhere else. For Douglass, among others, emigration represents a failure to do service to the race, to the cause of black men and women in slavery. It is an assertion of self against race, of self against manhood, of self against nation: remember, if you can't be a man here, in America, you can't be a man anywhere else. 'By changing your place', he concludes in the *Frederick Douglass Paper*, again in 1852, 'you don't change your character' (Douglass 1950: 173).

Exposed to 'charges of apostasy and betrayal' – charges coming from former colleagues like Douglass and benefactors like William Jay – Crummell was forced to take on the question of racial types, manhood and nation, questions which run throughout his speeches and writings (Moses 1992: 86). In 'The Progress and Prospects of the Republic of Liberia', a speech delivered at the annual meeting of the New York State Colonization Society on 9 May 1861, Crummell summarised his vision of the limit imposed on black men in American society. 'We cannot, it is true,' he began, 'make great pretensions':

> our training and culture have been exceedingly imperfect. We have been deprived of many of our rights in this country. We have been debarred from many of those privileges and prerogatives which develop character into manhood, and mastery, and greatness. Still we have not been divorced from your civilization. We have not been cut off from the lofty ideas and the great principles which are the seeds of your growth and greatness, political, intellectual, and ecclesiastical. ... And hence I feel desirous that those enterprising and Christian men here, who are looking abroad for new homes, and other fields of labor, should join us in Africa, for the regeneration of that continent. (Crummell 1992: 173)

Not much chance, then, of being a man where you are if you happen to be black in America (or, indeed, in England where William Jay had been too embarrassed to let Crummell call on him).[1] Ever since *David Walker's Appeal* in 1829, the dream of a racial polity, the goal of an unfettered manhood, had been the political ambition of men such as Edward Blyden, Martin Delany and Crummell. Echoing Blyden's conviction 'that the Negro can never attain in this country to the distinction of true manhood', both Crummell and Delany concluded, bitterly, that they would never be allowed to be men in the United States – a conclusion that led them to redefine, or try to, the boundaries of what it meant to be a free black man in racist America (Blyden 1971: 12). Certainly, manliness and the struggle for a black, Christian nationality appear here to be worth the price of apostasy and betrayal. Debarred but not divorced from Anglo-Saxon culture and civilisation, excluded but not cut off from those lofty ideas and great principles, Crummell felt compelled to overcome that separation by travelling to Liberia – a nation founded by the American Colonization Society in 1820 for the purpose of encouraging free black Americans to return to their African 'homeland'. When he arrived in Liberia, Crummell expressed nothing but commitment to the Liberian cause: 'The failure of this type or the destruction of *that* form, is no prevention of nature's upward reaching', he wrote in 1862, outlining his belief that it was 'the plain duty and the manifest destiny of LIBERIA' to discover 'a higher type of true nationality' (Crummell, cited in Moses 1992: 103). For Crummell, in his neo-Lamarkian approach to history, that higher type was the guarantee of the lasting future of the black race. If Liberia, Crummell continues, is destined to make a distinct contribution to 'the great commonwealth of humanity', then it must both aspire to 'the cultivation of MEN' and take as its model the most civilised nations: Greece and Rome. Only then, Crummell concludes, will the world witness 'the grateful vision of a manly, noble, and complete African nationality' (Crummell, cited in Moses 1992: 108, 110).

Against the backdrop of this vision, Crummell begins to extrapolate, hypothesise, the true image and meaning of African nationality. In particular, what emerges through Crummell's thinking in the 1860s is a connection between a 'higher type of true nationality' and a black type itself guaranteed by its capacity for imitation. In other words, running together the ideas of nation, race and imitation, Crummell will identify black men as true representatives of nationality in so far as he typifies them as true imitators. In this he was not only reversing the meaning of assimilation beloved by Abolitionists such as Douglass, but challenging the prevailing views of nineteenth-century race psychology on the Negro's credulous suggestibility, his dangerously uninhibited, unconscious emulation of whites. In answer to the 'Douglass Dictum', published in the *North Star* in 1849 – 'We can be remodified, changed, and assimilated, but never extinguished', 'we are here, and ... this is our country' – Crummell will refer to the African man as the exemplary instance of racial survival and to Africa as the perfect place for the assimilation and remodification of Western civilisation. In answer to a familiar point – 'Everyone has heard', writes Herbert Spencer in 1876, 'of the ways in which Negroes, when they have opportunities, dress and swagger in grotesque mimicry of the whites' – Crummell will echo and revise Count de Gobineau's view, in *Essais sur l'inegalité des races humaines*, that black men are imitative, artistic in intelligence, and that imitation represents the surest sign of advanced civilisation and culture (Spencer 1893: 81). Crummell's opposition to the widely held (post-emancipation) views of race psychologists such as Joseph Dowd or J. M. Mecklin[2] – that the Negro's 'natural suggestibility' betrays a compulsive conformity to 'social imitation' typifying the 'massing of unassimilated groups' – will lead him to describe black imitation as a prescient sign not only of black future posterity but of a sublimely adaptive response to the legacies of slavery (Dowd 1914: 609). The distinction here, between a slavish and superior form of imitation, will prove crucial not only to Crummell's writings on Africa and black nationality but, upon his return to America, his critique of America's post-reconstruction treatment of blacks.

Indeed, he will transfer the racist distinction between inferior and superior forms of imitation onto a distinction between pure and impure black types, between mulattoes and 'pure blood' Negroes. In answer to the question: Which black men are destined for future superiority? What black type?, Crummell will draft one of his most important statements on Liberian national policy. (And a first step in a sustained critique – perhaps a deconstruction – of racist concepts of imitation.) On 26 June 1870, Crummell addresses the Common Council and the Citizens of Monrovia, the governing body of Liberia. His speech, 'Our National Mistakes and the Remedy for Them', prepared three years earlier to mark Liberia's Day of National Independence, expresses Crummell's concern at what he sees as the nation's failure to live up to his ideals. No longer is Liberia a land where dreams come true, where visions are gratefully awaited, where black nationalists are noble, manly and free. Liberia cannot be that if its rulers, or colonists, fail to exploit a new and powerful iconography of the *native* as type, as imitator. '*One great mistake of the people of Liberia*', Crummell declares, telling the truth as he sees it to his audience, is the '*neglect of our native population*' as a 'future element of society' (Crummell 1992: 176–7). Preaching to his listeners, he accuses the citizens of Monrovia and their leaders of blindness, of failing to recognise (his word) 'the native man' as a vital, national resource, a recognition 'which is desirable, as well as for our needs, as for his good' (ibid.). For 'here is a MAN', he continues, 'who, however rude and uncultivated', however simple and uncivilised, symbolises the future triumph of the race over the 'ghastly burial of centuries' (ibid.). If only we can see our manhood through him, use him, even, to model our future needs and desires, then we, too, can learn how to overcome the traumas of adversity and despair, the painful legacy of 'servitude and oblivious degradation' (ibid.). And if, as some assert, he is primitive, rude or savage, without the benefit of 'letters' or civilisation, that is no matter, for here is a man destined to last, a man 'prophetic of a lasting future'. But why? Because he is imitative: an imitator (and therefore an ideal resource for imperialist exploitation as slave labour). Crummell goes on:

> In his character you see nothing stolid, repulsive, indomitable. On the other hand he is curious, mobile, imitative. He sees your superiority, and acknowledges it by copying your habits. He is willing to serve you; and, after being in your service, he carries home with him the 'spoils', which he has gathered in your family, by observation and experience; which makes him there a superior fellow to his neighbour. (Crummell 1992: 184)

What, we might ask, is the connection between Liberia's failure to recognise this 'higher type of nationality' and that future, masculine ideal embodied in the native's ability to copy – to mime – 'our' image? Decimate his soul, engulf his culture, you cannot, in Crummell's view, 'destroy the native'. He may be 'gross, sordid, and sensual', having 'cast aside the habiliments of civilized life' and 'the fine harmonies and the grand thought of the English tongue', but, being slavishly imitative by nature, the native is able to repeatedly refigure and ennoble himself by carrying home with him your image as spoils (ibid.: 188, 191). It is no wonder that Crummell identifies a failure to 'exploit' that native resource as a failure of economic and public policy; and no wonder that he should insist that Liberia 'must undertake the moulding and fashioning of this fine material of native mind and character' if it is to succeed as a black imperialist nation (ibid.: 191). Whether as a racial ideal, or type, native imitation is obviously good for the soul in bringing Liberians together and teaching them the true meaning of their imperial destiny; for, without native imitativeness, Liberia cannot represent itself to itself as the ideal type of nationality. Revising Spencer's dismissal of black imitation from grotesque mimicry to vital resource, Crummell thus ties the idea of imitation to a political and evolutionary narrative about African racial types. With that shift in perception, we can see the extent to which the liberatory potential of the native for Liberia emerges as that nation's need to be confirmed by an ideal, imitative type.

And yet, if Liberia's destiny is simply, and triumphantly, to replicate itself through the native as imitator – a type whose capacity for imitation guarantees its hardihood – in Liberian settler society, by contrast, colonisation has resulted in a ruling 'ephemeral caste' able to guarantee neither itself nor the future of the nation. Crummell's stress on the need for Americo-Liberians to recognise, and benefit from, the native as imitator comes from an attempt to make Liberia realise his vision of its national destiny as a 'pure' black nation. As though Liberia's failure to see the appeal of the native, a blindness peculiar to its leaders, is, for Crummell, down to the confused and undefined presence of a 'mixed multitude', or mixed breed: the mulattoes. At the same time, by saying how much Liberia has lost sight of its future embodied in the native, Crummell's romantic and nationalist appeal to 'our' Liberia tends to blame mulattoes for those national mistakes: addressing with some irony his mulatto fellow citizens as 'a people of Negro blood', as 'kindred in race and blood', Crummell ends his sermon with the exhortation – 'This is the time of the Negro!' (ibid.: 191, 193). For, having an improper knowledge of the native as type, mulattoes, it seems, can only be a threat to this future time of the Negro, the direct antithesis of its realisation.

A lot has been written about Crummell's almost pathological loathing for the lighter-skinned members of the Americo-Liberian ruling minority, men whom he accused of being a 'filthy class ... who hate the Negro more intensely than any slave-dealer at the South ever did – men whose whole life has been spent crushing out black men' (Crummell, cited in Moses 1992: 160). At other, similarly exposed and revealing moments, he would complain, perhaps ambiguously, that mulattoes were 'as Negro hating as the voters of Memphis' for whom 'Your true black man is inferior, and can't do anything' (Crummell, cited in Moses ibid.: 160). In becoming a witness, then, for the great power to be gained from the native as imitator – Colonise, recognise him, and Liberia has a future; don't, and Liberia will be doomed to 'the vast burial of centuries' – Crummell was also acting as a prosecuting witness against the mulatto as a degraded type of black nationality. (Figuring racial type in terms of destiny, Crummell was unable to picture a political or racial future for mulattoes other than a form of degenerate 'bastardy': not being party to that model figure – 'true [black] men' like himself – they were condemned out of hand as the type that devalues, disfigures, a properly *black* national future (Crummell

1992: 97, 87).)[3] His thinking on types is, in other words, nothing less than a fantasy of caste viciously wed to the image of itself as an ideal constituency. And, as a form of political discourse, that imaging can zoom in on the native only through the lens of caste exclusion.

Addressing his audience of mainly mulattoes on a day of national celebration, I suspect that Crummell's line of reasoning produced many conflictual responses: from racial affirmation to a genuine *political* foreclosure, or a bemused, or angry, denial – the latter perhaps signified by muted applause, a weary shuffling of feet. If Crummell's version of black nationalism – his dream of black men as a representative ideal, or model, of nationality – is based on black men as racial imitators, a habit of thinking that saw itself threatened by those vilified and despised types – the mulattoes – I can't help wondering whether that relation between racial type, imitation and nation can itself only be thought *imitatively*: that is, through a necessarily blind imitation of a racist concept of imitation? As if Crummell's thinking was defined by an inability to resist imitating – or, at least, uncritically reproducing – a racist concept of race purity that unwittingly starts to undo, to disfigure, his already imitative dream of black male superiority. At first sight, Crummell's ideas on the African as imitator reads like a reprise of nineteenth-century American race psychology. In M. Baldwin's 1895 *Mental Development in the Child and the Race*, for example, black psychic life is presented as unconsciously driven by a need to assimilate which, in its disavowal of time, is condemned to live in a perpetual present like a child. Further, unlike the white child who learns, via a process of psychic sympathy, that other people's bodies 'have experiences *in them* such as mine has' – 'they are also *me's*: let them be assimilated to my *me* copy' – the black child is, according to Baldwin, too ejective, has too much of the 'outside thrown in', and is therefore open to the devoid, and dangerously suggestive, arena of crowds (Baldwin 1895: 355). Like the 'undeveloped child, the parrot, the idiot, the hypnotic, the hysterical', black children can only imitate those images and emotions which the outside throws in, an imitativeness, which registers as a desire to be *similar* (ibid.: 349). Similarly, for Dowd, in *The Negro in American Life*, 'the Negro's extraordinary imitativeness', his ability to personate and assimilate other parts and characters, is linked to an hypnotic or somnambulistic state which is always more alter than ego, an imitativeness which he uses to explain black 'self-abasement' and 'submissiveness' (Dowd 1927: 407).

Despite, then, substituting manliness and culture for these ideas of regressive evolution, Crummell continues to reproduce imitation as a racial trait defining blackness. That mimicry, I want to suggest, was not only in itself deeply equivocal but also troubled and troubling. We ought perhaps to read here, beyond those categorial assertions of racial purity and impurity, an almost obsessive concern with the limits of racial identity whose achingly delusive quality can only be figured in assertions of type and anti-type, disfigured models and suspect simulations. Perhaps it was the bitter, desperate experience of being typed by mulattoes as a Negro that taught him to be angry in this way; perhaps this is why Crummell strives to undo the links between certain racial types and black (national) destiny. But it is also true that he was ultimately unable to give up thinking racially about types, a particular way of imagining identity that perpetuates the deepest of racial divisions. It is indeed telling that, in his quest for black nationality, the very simplest of questions as to why blacks would want to imitate whites should involve Crummell in so much personal cost. After Liberia had degenerated, in 1871, into a racial civil war fought between rival mulatto and black factions, Crummell left hurriedly for Sierra Leone, in fear of his life. Eventually, he returns to America. Setting sail for Boston in March, 1872, that journey all but ended his quest for the romance of Africa, even though, as well shall see, it soon led to a new, altogether more radical connection between race and imitation.

Upon his return to America having been appointed, in 1872, rector to St. Mary's Chapel, Washington, DC (the cultural capital of black America at this time), Crummell's growing concerns over the political struggle for black civil rights become particularly provocative on the question of racial and civic 'assimilation'. Undoubtedly, there are historical, and personal, reasons for why this should be the case. But in an 1875 Thanksgiving sermon, aptly named 'The Social Principle among a People and Its Bearing on Their Progress' (a text which had originally been prepared as an attack on Liberian settler society), Crummell makes an explicit connection between the continuing exclusion of Afro-Americans from 'the real life of the nation' – an exclusion which, he argues, 'constitutes us "a nation within a nation"' – and the 'need for us all to hold on to the remembrance that *we* are "colored men", and not to forget it!' (Crummell 1995: 32, 38). 'The only place I know of in this land where you can "forget you are colored"', he continues, 'is the grave!' (ibid.: 35). Alongside this urging of black men not to forget who they are, Crummell articulates the following demand: America's '*white* population should forget, be made to forget, that we are *colored* men!' (ibid.: 40). Linking black remembrance to white forgetting, Crummell's vision of cultural equality between the races proposes that for blacks to be the cultural equal of whites, the latter must be forced to forget themselves as white, as racial *types*. Only then, it seems, can blacks be truly, freely black, and whites escape the violent legacy of racism. Whites, as 'the *people of the land*', must 'be forced to forget all the facts and theories of race', he states, facts and theories which, in vilifying black men and women as perverse and parasitical imitators, have also exiled them from the real life of the nation (ibid.: 40, 39). If whites can be made to forget 'all the theories of [black] inferiority', he continues, then such cynical assumptions 'will pass, with wonderful rapidity, into endless forgetfulness' (ibid.: 39). But, given that whites have not yet forgotten such habits of thinking, blacks must force them to forget through sheer force of moral character. Years later, in 1895, he will announce: 'Moral qualities are prophecies' (ibid.: 181). Like the native as imitator, then, Afro-Americans must learn to draw on the enormous and generative power of their capacity for imitation if they are to transform 'the childhood' of their nationality into the 'healthful maturity' of nationhood (ibid.: 47).[4] Only then will black recollection, driven by ghosts of times past, be allowed to reimagine its hopes and aspirations for a redemptive future as part of America's supposedly real national life.

The most striking example of Crummell's rhetoric of those hopes and aspirations is to be found in a sermon he delivered in 1877 at St Mary's on 'The Destined Superiority of the Negro'. Albeit brief, in this address Crummell explores the typing of blacks as an unassimilable sign – or type – within American race relations through the slanders of 'race psychology': one of those insistent, arrogant theories he hoped that whites would forget. A theory that, as we've already seen, made black imitation into a synonym for a credulous, hypnotically regressive conformity to social copy possessing the *least* inhibition and the *most libido* and *philia* – the most insistent and the most degraded capacity for friendship and love. 'Savages copy quicker, and they copy better', observes Walter Bagehot, in his 1875 text, *Physics and Politics*, offering us a glimpse into why blacks end up being repeatedly figured in these discourses as those whose sole life activity is *copying* – apishly, slavishly – their masters. Because, for Crummell, such theories disregard the role imitation plays in the evolution of great cultures and civilisations, because they decry – slanderously, dismissively – black imitation 'as the simulation of a well-known and grotesque animal', they are totally impervious to why black men, being imitators *par excellence*, can serve as models, ideals, or paragons of universal culture (ibid.: 50). In so far as the cultures and civilisations of the 'two great, classic nations' – Greece and Rome – 'were stratified with the elements of imitation; and that Roman culture is but a copy of a foreign and alien civilization', Crummell declares, then the Negro, whom he variously defines as pliant, mobile, assimilative and plastic, will, given the time and opportunity, not only learn to imitate this great, classic capacity for imitation, but he will go on to develop an 'imitative art' to 'rival them both' (ibid.: 50, 51). Because whites seem totally unable to imagine this future imitative art, blinded by the racism they have indulged in, unconscious of their own histories of imitation, they have resorted to the complacency of typecasting blacks as utterly absorbed in the appearances of whites as superior types.

That oversight, though somewhat more complicated than I am suggesting here, is, for Crummell, symptomatic of a wider failure to accurately assess the virtues of endless striving and sacrifice, the anxieties and aspirations and loving scrutiny of others, which, he believes, mark black desires for imitative assimilation. In the following long passage, which I cite in full, Crummell not only dismisses the racist rhetoric of the psychologists but sets out why, for him, imitation and uplift go together:

> But has this race any of those other qualities, and such a number of them, as warrants the expectation of superiority? Are plasticity, receptivity, and assimilation among his constitutional elements of character?
>
> So far as the first of these is concerned there can be no doubt. The flexibility of the Negro character is not only universally admitted; it is often formulated into a slur. The race is possessed of a nature more easily moulded than any other class of men. Unlike the stolid Indian, the Negro yields to circumstances, and flows with the current of events. Hence the most terrible afflictions have failed to crush him. His facile nature wards them off, or else, through the inspiration of hope, neutralises their influence. Hence, likewise, the pliancy with which, and without losing his distinctiveness, he runs into the character of other people; and thus bends adverse circumstances to his own convenience; thus, also, in a measurable degree, linking the fortunes of his superiors to his own fate and destiny.
>
> These peculiarities imply another prime quality, anticipating future superiority; I mean imitation. This is also universally conceded, with, however, a contemptuous fling, as though it were an evidence of inferiority. But Burke tells us that 'imitation is the second passion belonging to society; and this passion', he says, 'arises from much the same cause as sympathy'.[5] This forms our

> manners, our opinons, our lives. It is one of the strongest links of society. Indeed, all civilization is carried down from generation to generation, or handed over from the superior to the inferior, by means of this principle. A people devoid of imitation are incapable of improvement, and must go down; for stagnation of necessity brings with it decay and ruin.
>
> On the other hand, the Negro, with a mobile and plastic nature, with a strong receptive faculty, seizes upon and makes over to himself, by imitation, the better qualities of others. First of all, observe that, by a strong assimilative tendency, he reduplicates himself, by attaining both the likeness of and an affinity to the race with which he dwells; and then, while retaining his characteristic peculiarities, he glides more or less into the traits of his neighbours. Among Frenchmen, he becomes, somewhat, the lively Frenchman; among Americans, the keen, enterprising American; among Spaniards, the stately, solemn Spaniard; among Englishmen, the solid, phlegmatic Englishman. (ibid.: 50)

Whatever the combination of features attributed to imitation, it is universally admitted, Crummell notes, that blacks are superior imitators, with a unique, receptive capacity to mime the likenesses, to assimilate the fortunes, of others. Perhaps most typically enigmatic of all is the Negro's curious ability to invest himself with the possibility of a future by assimilating the accents, gestures and national identities of others. ('Among Frenchmen, he becomes, somewhat, the lively Frenchman; among Americans, the keen, enterprising American; among Spaniards, the stately, solemn Spaniard; among Englishmen, the solid, phlegmatic Englishman'.) One is struck by how definitely Crummell articulates his belief here that race mimicry marks the Negro out as the ideal type of nationality. The Negro's mobile, plastic nature has been, he reminds us, his 'grand preservative' in 'all the lands of his thraldom' (ibid.: 51). Imitation, it seems, saves. And in this vision of redemptive suffering, it doesn't seem to matter that black men copy; what matters is who? As a technique for survival, representing life for some and death for others, the Negro's imitative art has, over time, not only set him apart from those other, more impassive and so self-destructive races, prone to decay and ruin – the 'stolid Indian', for example[6] – but it has ensured that black nationality, in the face of terrible afflictions, will not be buried in 'the outstretched graveyards which occupy the sites of departed nations' (ibid.: 44). Even if 'the wrecks of nations lie everywhere upon the shores of time', he continues, there will always be other, exemplary races and nations, driven by a mimetic desire to assimilate the qualities of others – 'great nations' like Greece and Rome, great races like the Negro (ibid.: 44, 50).

Accordingly, the Negro's progress through discipline and trial, however terrible or cruel, reveals the true meaning of his 'future distinction': even in the lands of his thraldom, the fact would remain that his desire for mimesis (his desire to mime) read allegorically, analogically, and above all, typologically, expresses infinite possibilities (ibid.: 51). Whether taken, therefore, as the sign of a superior temporal destiny, or as the repetition of a racial destiny that precedes him, being imitative the Negro will never pass into the oblivion of racial stolidity, nor will he ever stagnate, losing, in the process, the means to civilisation and nationality. It would be sadly ironic, then, if blacks themselves missed the lessons of that positioning and failed to grasp the moral insight that comes from being in the position of both servile imitators and future masters. Putting a spin on the fall of empires and of peoples as proof of a cyclical, upwards movement of history, it clearly doesn't matter to Crummell that racial imitation can be both retrogressive in one instance and progressive in the next. Even though he encodes both movements as racial, the moral nature of black imitation is frequently emphasised, as against its demoniac or bestial typecasting. As if, in moving beyond type to become an exemplary archetype of the typical, black men could only enjoy, rather than be troubled by, the moral privilege of entering into and seizing the characters of others. As if, in reduplicating himself 'by attaining both the likeness of and an affinity to the race with which he dwells', the black man did not terrify and repel the French, the Spaniards, the English and Americans. In touting this rising black imaging, Crummell is, of course, careful to distinguish between likeness and affinity, racial quality and transference, i.e. all those possibilities of corruption between what is being represented and what is being reproduced. (Years later, in 1885, he will continue to insist that 'Every race of people has its special instincts, carries in its blood its distinctive individuality. This peculiar element is its own and exclusive possession, and is incapable of *transference*' (ibid.: 157, my italics).)

Yet the question remains why he postulates this drive to assimilate the racial traits of others, to be the same *as* the other, only then to imply that that other is really a reduplication of *myself*, or, in principle at least, to allow the possibility that an identity construed in and by an affinity for parody and fiction, by a performative desire to be other than itself, might have possibly contagious consequences for a concept of self-possession as such. If, for Crummell, black masculinity can never be identical to itself or with prospective repetitions of itself, it is because that identity is always oriented toward the future of its own repetition, ever driven toward a better version of itself *as* other. At least one thing, then, would be paradoxically self-evident: the black man imitates everybody except himself; and in this he faithfully reproduces – ensures – his superiority *as* a black man. But, and crucially, it is not black but European, Christian civilisation which continues to determine – to legitimate – the future worth and value of imitation for Crummell. (As a future identity, it seems, black men can only attain a white – as against a black – identification of themselves; indeed, in this prototypical identification with whiteness – a foundational culture and tradition which can be neither avoided nor eluded – it appears whiteness is the one racial identity which does not need to mediate, to copy, or to type, itself.)

I would like to explore, in the remainder of this chapter, what it would mean for black men to begin to take on this aporia as a way of purging, even purifying, that fraught image of themselves. In Edward Blyden's extraordinary *Christianity, Islam and the Negro Race*, first published in 1887, for example, the 'incubus of imitation' is not only viewed as opposed to the search by black men for a 'respectable manhood'; imitation is also what psychically prevents blacks from acquiring a true '*difference*' from whites: 'an imitator,' Blyden concludes, 'never rises above a mere copyist' (Blyden 1967: 351, 38). In an argument remarkably prophetic of Frantz Fanon's on cultural racism and black identity (the subject of my next chapter), Blyden argues that 'from the lessons he everyday receives', the Western, Christianised black man is taught to 'secure outward conformity to the appearance of the dominant race' and so to assimilate the racist 'caricatures and misrepresentations' of Western culture (ibid.). Forever 'striv[ing] after whatever is most unlike himself and most alien to his peculiar tastes', the Christian black man 'unconsciously imbibes the conviction that to be a great man he must be like the white man' (ibid.: 351, 37). Consequently, Western-educated blacks, unlike African Muslims, 'never feel at home', but 'in the depth of their being, they always feel themselves strangers in the land of their exile, and the only escape from this feeling is to escape from themselves' (ibid.: 77). As if in answer to Douglass' dictum that 'individuals emigrate – nations never', Blyden's analysis of how culture intrudes on the black psyche suggests African-Americans are already, impassably, in exile from themselves. No surprise, then, that he should propose that the black psyche can only be at home, or *heimlich*, in the refuge of the fatherland, Africa.

Or that a return to Africa should be presented as a cure for the 'fatal contagion of a mimic or spurious Europeanism' (ibid.: 352). If Christian blacks, in their psychic disunity, serve as a general emblem for black misidentity, for Blyden 'the superior manliness and *amour propre* of Negro Mohammedans' represent an alternative black cultural identity (ibid.: 13–14). In a perhaps inaccurate, but nonetheless revealing, commentary on Islamic attitudes to representation, Blyden compares the Muslim 'prohibition of all representations' with Christian 'models of imitation' (ibid.). The Muslim ban on images, he observes, has resulted in a manliness capable of cultural and psychic self-possession, whereas the black Christian's 'mimetic faculty' has 'destroyed. ... his self-respect, and made him the weakling and creeper which he appears in Christian lands' (ibid.: 14–15). Such a man, Blyden continues, is 'not brought up – however he may desire it – to be the companion, the equal, the comrade of the white man, but his imitator, his ape, his parasite', adding that, in his aspiration to be like the white man, the Christian Negro is 'less, worse than nothing' (ibid.: 37). He is 'a sick man's dream' (ibid.).

The cure for that sick dreamwork of culture, the self-alienating fantasy it represents is, for Blyden, an anti-imitative Islamic Africa. 'How shall we make our "lives sublime"?' he asks, concluding his inaugural lecture as President of Liberia College on 5 January 1881. 'Not by imitating others', he advises, 'but by doing well our own part as they did theirs' for, in the 'lofty manhood of nation-building, that part will be attained' (ibid.: 92, 93). Rather than follow Crummell's elevation of imitation as the source of all that is *original* in European and classical culture, and as the model, the ideal type for black nationality, Blyden thus proposes an African manliness that cannot be represented and therefore exiled, subjugated and oppressed by white ideals and images, by the sick dream of psychical, and racial, assimilation. The dismissal, or reinflection, here, of the race psychology view that the Negro is naturally imitative underlies Blyden's attempt, throughout *Christianity, Islam and the Negro Race*, to end the exile of African-Americans by liberating them from their psychic enslavement to white culture. If Blyden's notion of imitation nonetheless continues to type black imitators in racially divisive and exclusive terms, that is because, recalling Crummell, he also believes that mulattoes are more prone to imitate white culture than 'genuine' blacks. In a letter to the Secretary of the American Colonization Society, dated 19 October 1874, Blyden describes the inner life of mulattoes as 'always restless and dissatisfied' in their desire for complete racial assimilation with whites (Blyden, cited in Lynch 1967: 108). Accordingly, genuine blacks must be defended against those dissatisfied types – the mulattoes who, being half-white, are more prone to imitate the caricatures and misrepresentations of white culture – if they are to achieve nationality and manhood. Even though he found exceptions – of Douglass he wrote, 'He is strongly Negro, although of mixed blood. His genius and power come evidently from the African side of his nature' – Blyden's at times ludicrous notion of race instinct or ancestry only serves to fuel what his biographer Hollis Lynch refers to as a 'paranoid hatred of mulattoes' (ibid.: 108, 129). One wonders what Blyden made of that other prominent 'mixed-blood' intellectual, W. E. B. Du Bois, who not only deepened and refined Crummell's racialised notion of imitation, but extended that analysis to the psychic divisions of African-American identity in his 1903 classic, *The Souls of Black Folk*.

In Du Bois' famous eulogy on Crummell, written a year after Crummell's death and delivered at Tuskegee Institute in 1899 under the title 'Strivings of a Negro for the Higher Life', the question of black psychic assimilation becomes part of a wider imaging of Crummell as a soul doubly and impassably self-divided, split by the varying tides of intolerance and dissolution that, at key moments, overwhelmed the moral certainties of the life as lived. In 'Alexander Crummell', first published in *Souls*, that inner divide, or double consciousness ('two unreconciled strivings; two warring ideals in one dark body'), becomes Du Bois' vehicle for typing Crummell's life as a 'world wandering of a soul in search of itself', in whose desperate, ghostly 'passing' that soul 'has missed its duty' (Du Bois 1992: 27). Exploring Crummell's exile, his 'weird pilgrimage' to the 'wild fever-cursed swamps of West Africa', Du Bois draws a picture of Crummell's life as one 'ever haunted by the shadow of a death that is more than death', a life nevertheless refusing to give in to hate, doubt, or despair despite Crummell being forced to live, divided against himself, within the Veil of racism (ibid.). Such a scenario accounts for why Du Bois, drawing on an Afro-American historical typology of exile and diaspora, depicts Crummell as a martyred pilgrim, as a world wandering ghost: 'like some grave shadow he flitted by those halls' and 'haunted the streets' (ibid.: 24). Why? Because by the end of the 1890s, in the anti-black period known as Reconstruction, Crummell's politics of 'protest and prophecy', his prescient, even evangelical, belief in the future, imitative superiority of the Negro, has been exposed as the deluded pursuit of ghosts. In 'Of Alexander Crummell', therefore, while primarily engaged in epideictic eulogy, Du Bois is also carefully taking stock of Crummell's intellectual legacy. In response to Crummell's sacred notions of prescience and imitation, for example, Du Bois presents a secular, humanistic notion of *Bildung* – an active, creative realisation of human potentialities, an ideal of a life dedicated to organic growth and aesthetic creativity, enriched and ennobled by the life of the mind. In particular, substituting *Bildung* for imitation allows Du Bois to reject Crummell's 'unbending righteousness' (for which he had become – rather infamously – known), to reject his too guarded a notion of self, his attempt to assimilate, without sacrificing himself to the variety, richness and diversity of experience (the very moral qualities which Crummell had earlier defined as the source of black imitation). In short, if in the spring of 1895, when they first met, Du Bois felt there was a certain psychic empathy between himself and Crummell, a shared humanistic ideal of black enlightenment as well as a shared sense of alienation and despair, by 1899 he was less sure that Crummell's moral ideal of black civilisationism was the best way of securing manhood and citizenship in America. On the one hand, despite reading Crummell's life as both cynosure and archetype for an enlightenment ideal of black political leadership (an ideal he will term the 'Talented Tenth'), Du Bois' search for manhood in America is, in *Souls*, primarily presented as an aesthetics of personality rather than an obsessive concern with racial types and images, black racial purity and nationhood. On the other, the influence of Du Bois' aesthetic concept of *Bildung* on both the ideals and image of the 'New Negro' which emerged in the 1920s, not only ensured that this artistic and literary movement defined itself in anti-imitative terms but caused it to reject out of hand any notion of a black mimetic faculty.

It was a bizarre reversal. For Alain Locke, writing in the Editorial of *The New Negro*, first published in 1925, the stereotypical image of the Negro in the American mind is the result of 'historical fictions' imposed on blacks (Locke 1925: 21). 'Through a sort of protective social mimicry forced upon him by the adverse circumstances of dependence', the Negro, he writes, has learnt a 'psychology of imitation and implied inferiority' which has inhibited his creativity (ibid.: 22). 'More a formula than a human being,' he continues, '[his] shadow, so to speak, has been more real to him than his personality' (ibid.). For Locke, then, the New Negro's radical 'self-dependence' requires a new 'transformed and transforming psychology', one that is no longer tied to the old relations of dependent imitation (ibid.: 25). In an important critical reconstruction of this 'reconstruction', 'The Trope of a New Negro and the Reconstruction of the Image of the Black', Henry Louis Gates, Jr., writing, it would seem, against Locke, argues that this reinscription of the black as imitative type was itself, paradoxically enough, part of an assimilative psychology of racial imitation, an argument which, in ways that we have already examined, poses imitation in opposition to racial authenticity:

> If the New Negroes of the Harlem Renaissance sought to erase their received racist image in the Western imagination, they also erased their racial selves, *imitating those they least resembled* in demonstrating the full intellectual potential of the black mind. ... Such was the extent to which this fantasy of indirect liberation ran. ... Claiming that the isolated, cultured, upper-class part stood for the potential of the larger black whole, it sought to *imitate* forms of Western poetry, 'translating', as it was put, the art of the untutored folk into a 'higher', standard English mode of expression, more compatible with the Western tradition. (Gates 1988: 148, my italics)

Accordingly, by rejecting those historical fictions of blacks as imitators, Locke and his followers have not only forgotten themselves as black (types?) but have unwittingly fallen victim to the imitative (white?) fantasy that they speak for the race as a whole. To be imitative, so the logic of this argument runs, represents a desire to be white, or at least amounts to a fraudulent claim to blackness. The fact that Gates and Locke share this opposition between imitation and race purity suggests that, for both men, imitation amounts to a failure to conserve and retain one's likeness, or kind, denoting a desire to be what you are not (the least resembled). That opposition is already a fantasy about the proper boundaries between ego and alter, self and image, white and black, and one which we've seen before.

Whereas for Crummell imitation represents a conservation rather than a dissolution of racial instincts, for Blyden, and several other commentators, imitation obliterates (since it erodes) racial difference. Either way, imitation becomes a figure for what closes the gap between the exemplary and the typical. While complicated, the attempt by Crummell, and others, to rewrite racist, stereotypical, images of black imitation amounts to an historical and aesthetic response to stereotypical discourses of black inferiority. While I understand, to go back to my earlier remarks, that one doesn't necessarily mimic in order to see oneself, or to see oneself as other, this idea of mimicry doesn't explain the relationship between white egos and black alters. If, as cultural property, blacks can only be typecast for their fervent scrutiny of the likenesses of others, perhaps a more complicated investment than a desire to copy is informing the symbolic theft, by whites, of black images. In countless scenes of white American culture captured by – and inscribing itself within – its own scenic fantasies, it appears that only whites, as a foundational model or founding term, can act as proper imitators.[7] 'There is an unwritten law in America that though white may imitate black', writes Jessie Faucet in her contribution to *The New Negro* anthology, 'The Gift of Laughter', 'black, even when superlatively capable, must never imitate white. In other words, grease-paint may be used to darken but never to lighten' (Faucet 1925: 48). That law ensures there can be no black metaphorical reversal of this edict without a dire iconoclasm: do not act *as* white (put on 'airs' as a black man) or you will end up looking like *this* (lynched and castrated) as the fanatical rise in race violence during this period underscored. Blacks, then, must not only suffer the anonymity of being imitated as types but, because of their slave heritage, they can only slavishly ape – as types – the images of others. It took the complex thinking of someone like Alexander Crummell to make possible another interpretation of black mimesis by reminding Afro-America that miming is not only a forceful, appropriative act leading to possession as well as dispossession, but that one also has an ethical and prescient value. When Crummell died, at the height of Jim Crow in America, unwilling to resign himself to a future without black imitation, unable to renounce a future that would do away with whiteness as a model, there was no more radical a gesture than a black man advocating a black imitation of white culture, of treating white images as the destined cultural property of a black inheritance.

Notes

1. According to Crummell's biographer, Wilson J. Moses:

   When Jay toured England in 1848 with his new bride, Crummell seems to have had difficulty even securing an interview. For the Jays to pay a social call on the Crummells would probably have been out of the question, but Crummell tried to arrange a personal meeting 'two or three times' and apparently even traveled to London in hopes of seeing his benefactor. (Moses 1992: 87)

2. In *Democracy and Race Friction*, for example, a book that was widely read and much quoted on its first publication in 1914, J. M. Mecklin describes black imitation as 'external and reproductive rather than assimilative and rational', as social or *ejective* in character rather than egotistical, or personal in form:

> From what we have seen of the highly suggestive and gregarious nature of the negro it is to be expected that he would be very imitative. ... But, as was to be expected in view of the difference in cultural levels, this imitation has been external and reproductive rather than assimilative and rational. The negro has imitated the forms and symbols of the white culture too often rather than its spirit and intent. ... This slavish imitation of the white, even to the attempted obliteration of physical characteristics, such as woolly hair, is almost pathetic and exceedingly significant as indicating the absence of feelings of race pride or race integrity. (Mecklin 1914: 98–9)

Consequently, because the Negro's social imitativeness is a copy of external and reproductive form rather than the imitative assimilation of ideas, it remains an unconscious or plastic psychological process rather than a conscious, or 'apperceptive process' of rational thought (ibid.: 52). The Negro's 'imaginal' way of thinking is, therefore, at the mercy of his emotions and appetites, which he finds more vivid than either morals or ideas. All of these things show the limitations of the Negro's faculty of the imagination, and are taken as evidence of the momentary impressions of his psychic life as well as the limits of his capacity for civilisation. Further, it is his greater susceptibility to the 'force' of crowd suggestion – made worse by his imitation of exterior fashion rather than inner character or custom – that explains the peculiar cast of his mind. For Joseph Dowd, writing in a discussion of G. Weatherby's 'The Racial Element in Social Assimilation', first published in 1916, the main reason for the 'moral retrogression of the Negro in America since emancipation' lies in the fact that

> wherever personal imitations are excluded by failure of one race to mingle freely with another, the excluded race is all the more susceptible to social imitation. It takes on an exaggerated and intensified interest in the suggestions of the crowd and on account of the inferiority and often demoralizing character of such suggestions it is made worse instead of better by the contact. I believe that the principles I am laying down explain the almost universal phenomenon of the degeneracy and dying out of inferior races in contact with the superior – a phenomenon which we observe in Africa, India, and Polynesia where the Caucasian has come in contact with the native population. These principles also explain the moral retrogression of the Negro in America since emancipation, the backward trend of many of our Indian population, and the moral peculiarities of the Jew. (Dowd 1916: 634)

In short, race psychology amounts to a reading of the black psyche as the *alter* of the white *ego* and sociality. For Dowd, the emancipation of slaves has occasioned, or let loose, the desires of an 'excluded' imitation which, because of its suggestibility, will prove delicate and difficult to harness: its lack of civility means it has no prototype or reserve. The freed slaves lack an historical synonym for free, civic, responsible existence. They are unmoored and, like crowds, dangerously so.

3. And he wasn't alone, either: his colleague at Liberia College, the West Indian intellectual, Edward Blyden, Professor of Greek and Latin, shared Crummell's 'hatred of mulattoes' and distaste for mulatto emigrants (Lynch 1967: 129). He described a dispute on College policy between himself and Crummell, on the one side, and the College's Executive Committee headed by Joseph Jenkins Roberts – a mulatto (who also happened to be a former premier of Liberia) – on the other, as a 'terrible conflict ... between the blacks and the confounded bastards' (Blyden, cited in Moses 1992: 159). Certainly, Blyden never stopped proposing the emigration of genuine Negroes only to Liberia, whom he preferred to the mongrel 'rubbish' and their desires for a black nationality. On 6 October 1869, in a letter to the Secretary of the New York Colonization Society, Blyden argued that 'mixed breeds' had 'feeble constitutions' and therefore should be discouraged from emigration (Blyden 1971: 188). For both men, mulattoes were seen as lacking in the virtues of hardiness and racial vitality necessary for emigration; and, being closer to whites, they were also seen as political opportunists – a 'conceited junto' – neither white nor black, who were more 'malignant' in their hatred of blacks 'than white men' (Crummell 1992: 87). For Crummell, the basis of their so called 'superiority' was not superior culture or attainments, but 'Bastardy' (ibid.). Seen in these terms, miscegenation, rather than slavery, emerges as the true aberration of caste. Neither Blyden, nor Crummell, ever stopped hating mulattoes *as* types, a prejudice which shapes both their political philosophy and theories of culture.

4. Similarly, in a remarkable 1885 address on 'The Need of New Ideas and New Aims for a New Era', given at Harper's Ferry with Frederick Douglass in attendance, Crummell, identifying what he terms 'an irresistible tendency in the Negro mind ... to settle down in the dismal swamps of dark and distressful memory', encourages his audience to no longer dwell 'morbidly and absorbingly on the servile past' (Crummell 1995: 121). In doing so he raises the moral and historical question of whether it was possible for Afro-Americans to define an elective, racially patriotic nationality without a forced, or unavoidable, reference to the memory of slavery. Employing a distinction between memory and recollection – memory is characterised by its passivity whereas recollection 'is the actual seeking of the facts – the painstaking endeavour of the mind to bring them back to their own consciousness' – Crummell warns his audience to concentrate on the future and not on the 'abiding recollection' of the past (ibid.: 123). At the same time, his key objection –

'not [to] the memory of slavery, but [to] the constant *recollection* of it' – placed him in the rather odd position of appealing to black men to retrieve their historic destiny through an act of forgetfulness, a fateful – but nonetheless preservative – decision undertaken as such. Not surprisingly, Douglass vigorously contested Crummell's argument.

5. The passage from Edmund Burke's 1757 *A Philosophical Enquiry into the Origin of Our Ideas of the Sublime and Beautiful*, London: Routledge, is as follows:

   > The second passion belonging to society is imitation, or, if you will, a desire of imitating, and consequently a pleasure in it. This passion arises from much the same cause with sympathy. For as sympathy makes us take a concern in whatever men feel, so this affection prompts us to copy whatever they do; and consequently we have a pleasure in imitating, and in whatever belongs to imitation merely as it is such, *without any intervention of the reasoning faculty*, but solely from our natural constitution, which providence has framed in such a manner as to find either pleasure or delight according to the nature of the object, in whatever regards the purposes of our being. It is by imitation far more than by precept that we learn every thing; and what we learn thus we acquire not only more effectually, but more pleasantly. This forms our manners, our opinions, our lives. It is one of the strongest links of society; it is a species of mutual compliance which all men yield to each other, without constraint to themselves, and which is extremely flattering to all. (ed. J. T. Boulton [London, 1958], p. 49, emphasis added)

6. I simply don't have the space here to go into any detail on the complex associations, in black cultural theory, with the figure of the Native American, associations which would lead us quite rapidly on to nineteenth-century ethnological opinion. That said, despite their obvious disagreements, both Crummell and Douglass seem to fall into anti-Irish and anti-Native American sentiments (few that they are), when debating the hardiness of the black 'race'.
7. Compare the observations of H. W. Odum, a white sociologist, describing a black southern revivalist meeting in *Social and Mental Traits of the Negro*, first published in 1910:

   > At church they are in sympathy with every word and motion of the preacher, and they are in sympathy with each other's movements. They sanction what the preacher has to say, whether they understand it or not, and their exclamations of assent include many regular forms of 'amens'. They nod, bow, their bodies sway to and fro according to the stage of the sermon, until yielding to the impulse there is a perfect harmony of bodily rhythm and a perfect rhythm of sympathetic feeling. So too, when the white man speaks to the Negroes, they

> assume from the beginning the attitude of approval and there is a distinct evidence of sympathy. So it is in most of the meetings if no personal interest is challenged, and many Negroes have been seen to nod their assent weakly to everything a white man was saying, though his total utterance was the abuse of the Negro in his political aspirings. Under the influence of music and dancing the Negro has little control over his body and feet, and when one foot has begun to 'pat' and beat time, it would indeed be an interesting problem to prevent others from joining in. An unconscious and sympathetic movement corresponds to each wave of rhythm in the music and to the movement of the fiddler. … Again the Negro easily adapts himself to various circumstances and a part of his imitation may be explained by noting the original element of sympathy that exists. (Odum 1910: 247)

Here the preacher's sermon invokes nothing more than the peculiarity of a certain *rhythmic*, hypnotic affect, which is the more contagious for being in conformity with the rhythmic phrases of music. The perfect harmonisation of the Negro's imaginal sympathy with the rhythms of words and music finds a perfect echo and reverberation in the words and movements of the preacher – the echo cannot be resisted but is yielded to like an 'impulse'. Again, Odum's reading is typological: it attests to a primitive and primordial engagement with language and music, where there is no distinction between ego and the world, no relay or gap between wish and its representation. In this instance, the black experience of religion is both compulsive – showing evidence of 'little control' – and mimetic. It is an experience of both the utmost receptivity and suggestibility, one in which the will is powerless, as is logic, for the force of this feeling comes over the Negro in waves, edging out all semblance of logic, and all hopes of 'political aspiring'. More worryingly, this sympathetic collapse of image and affect even goes, according to Odum, against the Negro's best interests (he cannot help but assent weakly to everything a white man says).

IV Frantz Fanon's War[1]

> One is always in the position of having to decide between amputation and gangrene. (James Baldwin, *Notes of a Native Son*, 1964)

In 1942, a seventeen year old patriot, loyal to the Free France of General de Gaulle, set out from Vichy-occupied Martinique to join the Allied Forces stationed in Dominica. That crossing, from citizenship to active service, from one occupying colonial power to another, was to prove fateful for the young Frantz Fanon. Distinguishing himself as a soldier fighting with the Allies in North Africa and then in Europe, Fanon returned to Martinique as a decorated, and disillusioned, hero of war. He had experienced, at first hand, the racist hostility not only of the French army but of the French people he had come to liberate. That hostility, as shocking as it was painful to the black soldiers who had served in Allied Armies, had a formative influence on Fanon's life and work. '*In Europe*', he writes in *Black Skin, White Masks*, first published in 1952, '*the black man* [*le Noir*] *is the symbol of evil* [*le Mal*]', a black devil from whom the Europeans, and especially European women, shrink in fright (Fanon 1967: 188, Fr. 152). The fear, Fanon acknowledges, is not feigned, and it speaks to a fantasy at the heart of European culture. 'But when we assert that European culture has an *imago* of the Negro which is responsible for all the conflicts that may arise', he concludes, 'we do not go beyond reality' (ibid.: 169).[2]

In this by now well-known passage from *Black Skin, White Masks*, Fanon runs the language of war into the language of psychoanalysis and psychiatry; more accurately, he shows up how these languages can be made to advance on the notion of conflict between two opposed, or warring, forces. At issue is the war between black and white men, certainly, but also – and perhaps more urgently for Fanon – the black man irrevocably and unforgettably at war with himself. That quasi-internal war, or wars, is there throughout, engaging Fanon's own war-time experience alongside his incessant conflicts with a range of psychoanalytic and politico-philosophical texts. In short, war is already installed in Fanon's thinking, a war that is endless and unconfined, neither internalised nor externalised – irresistible. It consists, in effect, of multiple fronts and frontiers as the war on the outside crosses over onto the inside, attacking other fronts. If, as Hegel says, there can be no self-consciousness without struggle, or conflict, for Fanon, black self-consciousness is already occupied by a foreign force, an inner divide or unconscious partition that forbids any advance, or counter-attack, in the black man. At the same time, those quasi-internal wars become inseparable from Fanon's uncovering of the aggression, the hatred, at the heart of cultural life. Every society, every collectivity, Fanon insists, must find a channel, an outlet, through which the forces accumulated in the form of aggression can be released. Every society, he continues, every collective, will find its own means of catharsis, be it in the form of war or children's games, racist murder or psychodrama (ibid.: 145).

It is central to the argument of *Black Skin, White Masks* that the imago, the fantasy, of the black man is there to allow a certain purging, a purifying, of European culture. That purification, its release of the accumulated forces that Fanon will struggle to understand and to name, works to petrify the black man – a petrifaction that puts Fanon on the track of the role played by prevalent cultural representations, by cultural exhibition, in the production and mediation of racist hatreds. The idea of exhibition, of looking and being looked at, has been basic to recent critical approaches to Fanon's work, many of which cite his by now well-known account of being shattered by the reflection of himself as terrible object: '"Dirty nigger!" Or simply, "Look, a Negro!"' 'The glances of the other', Fanon recalls, 'fixed me there ... I was indignant. I demanded an explanation. Nothing happened. I burst apart. Now the fragments have been put together again by another self' (ibid.: 109). Burst apart and splintered, trenched by a humiliation that sheers right through him, it may be that the process of writing *Black Skin, White Masks* played its own part in that putting back together, in the constructing of another self to reflect on the one that had been lost. To say this is to suggest that for Fanon – as for others – writing can be a form of reparation, of self and of world. It is also to say that such reparation may have to go through the structures of looking and being looked at – of being exhibited – identified throughout *Black Skin, White Masks*, a book which returns insistently, even symptomatically, to images of black men – and black soldiers – in mainstream American cinema.

It is, I want to suggest, through cinema that Fanon goes back to war. 'I cannot go to a film without seeing myself', he writes in 'The Lived Experience of the Black', the fifth chapter of *Black Skin, White Masks*. 'I wait for me. In the interval, just before the film starts, I wait for me. The people in the theatre are watching me, examining me, waiting for me' (ibid.: 140). 'On the screen', he continues elsewhere, 'the Negro faithfully reproduces that imago' – that is, the unconscious fantasy, the imago or image, of blackness as savage, bestial, biological (ibid.: 169). In other words, for Fanon, the screen becomes one way in which a culture can reflect, can make apparent, its unconscious fantasies, one way in which unconscious fantasy is realised in culture. In this sense, Fanon asks us to think about cinema as a form of both unconscious and cultural history, a record of the racist fantasies of the cultures in which it has a place. In this sense again, *Black Skin, White Masks* is making a key intervention into debates concerning psychoanalysis and culture, one that begins with Fanon's own traumatising or, in his words, petrifying, wait for himself on screen. 'I recommend the following experiment to those who are unconvinced', he writes in an important footnote to his discussion:

> Attend showings of a Tarzan film in the Antilles and in Europe. In the Antilles, the young Black Man identifies himself *de facto* with Tarzan against the negroes. This is much more difficult for him in a European theatre, for the rest of the audience, which is white, *automatically* identifies him with the savages on screen. It is a conclusive experience. The negro is aware that one is not black with impunity. (ibid.: 152–3; 1952: 124–5; t.m.)

On first reading this passage, it seems that the young black spectator behaves like any other man in the audience: he identifies, narcissistically, omnipotently, with the protagonist on screen. He is Tarzan, lording it over his world: the beasts and the blacks ever faithful to the lures of the image which appear to be giving him something, rather than taking something away. But Fanon is concerned, too, with how the pleasures of that identification can be interrupted by the apparent 'fit' between the white man on screen and the white man in the audience, a 'fit' which depends on the image of the black as that against which the white hero, the white spectator, defines himself. Once that 'fit' has been made, it is not only extremely unsettling for the black spectator; it also prevents that screen from ever being *just* a mirror. Suddenly, it is as if only whites are enabled and entitled to see their collective, narcissistic reflection – their courage and their contempt – enacted in culture, on screen. By contrast, blacks must learn to assemble themselves before scopic acts gushing with racist vituperation. In Europe, the black spectator is reflected back to himself as, or by, the black imago passing between audience and screen – an imago which, by capturing his image *automatically*, virtually petrifies the black man forced to see himself in it. Petrifies because, as Fanon puts it earlier, 'there is identification – that is, the young Negro [*le jeune Noir*] subjectively adopts a white man's attitude' (ibid.: 147; 120). The injuries suffered from that encounter unleash an internal war between who the young black man is and who he imagines himself to be. In other words, because he has identified himself as white, in so far as he does not think of himself as black, the black man is open to the hatred, the racist violence, carried by the imago on screen, in culture. Open not only on the outside, Fanon suggests, but on the inside, too.

It will prove to be a conclusive experience. If whiteness is culturally privileged, blackness remains petrified by this negative doubling, never quite getting over the shock of seeing what appears between itself and the screen. Either way, the appearance, in this highly charged encounter, of an ambivalently identified and identifying cultural imago, produces a specular doubling in the very act of whites looking at blacks looking at the screen. It is through the mechanism of this double bind that Fanon identifies the black man's war with himself, a war that he goes on to explore through the idea of cinema as a form of collective identification and collective catharsis. Fanon's references to cinema are scattered throughout *Black Skin, White Masks* in speculative, even tantalising, asides which hold something in reserve, which never quite deliver the argument clamouring to be made. In fact, one of the starting points for this chapter was a sense that these asides are essential to Fanon's understanding of – his appeal to – the concepts, and rhetorics, of war. Consider the following examples of rhetorical war, chosen at random from *Black Skin, White Masks*.

> The black man must wage his war on both levels [the economic and the epidermalisation of social inferiority]. (11)

> The Negro [*le Noir*] arriving in France will react against the myth of the *R*-eating man from Martinique. He will become aware of it, and he will really go to war against it. (21, 16)

> The field of battle being marked out, I entered the lists. (114)

> But it is in his corporeality that the Negro is attacked. It is as a concrete personality that he is lynched. (163)

> In order to achieve morality, it is essential that the black, the dark, the negro [*nègre*] vanish from consciousness. Hence a negro is forever in combat with his own image. (194; t.m.)

> There is war, there are defeats, truces, victories ...
>
> On the field of battle, its four corners marked by the scores of negroes hanged by their testicles, a monument is slowly being built that promises to be grandiose. (221–2; t.m.)

> The young Black men whom he knew there sought to maintain their alterity. Alterity of rupture, of conflict, of battle. (222, 180; t.m.)

> I find myself suddenly in a world in which things do evil; a world in which I am summoned into battle; a world in which it is always a question of annihilation or triumph. (228)

Through repeated acts of rhetorical war, the black man appears to be already at war with himself, with the imago of himself. In this estrangement of the black psyche by a fantasmatic unconscious, by a foreign body which displaces the self, the act of waging war becomes a metaphor, not only for Fanon's conflictual relationship with the imago of the black, but for his own ambivalent relationship to psychoanalysis and film (and, by extension, existential Marxism and Hegelian ontology).[3] As if this conflict, via the endless repetition of the figure of war in Fanon's text, represented a conflict he could neither avoid nor resolve. Thus Fanon wages war on at least two fronts, and they come together in one of the more elusive footnotes to 'The Negro and Psychopathology', the chapter in which Fanon engages most directly, and extensively, with psychoanalysis. 'There has been much talk of psychoanalysis in connection with the negro', Fanon writes, but, 'distrusting the ways in which it might be applied, I have preferred to call this chapter "The negro and psychopathology"'. 'I am thinking here', he continues in a footnote, 'particularly of the United States. See, for example, *Home of the Brave*' (ibid.: 151, 123; t.m.).

Released in France under the title *Je suis un nègre*, this film not only speaks directly to Fanon's unresolved, internal war, it also links his 'distrust' to a war contiguous with the uses and abuses of psychoanalysis. Two things struck me on first reading this passage.

On the one hand, Fanon's stated distrust of psychoanalysis, or its *applications* (the distinction may be crucial), seems to undermine the broader project of *Black Skin, White Masks* in so far as it sets out to use psychoanalysis as an interpretative and therapeutic tool to address the open secret of racism. 'Only a psychoanalytical interpretation of the black problem can lay bare the anomalies of affect', Fanon suggests in his Introduction to the book; that is, only psychoanalysis can start to address, to abreact, the vicissitudes of narcissistic self-hatred experienced by the black (ibid.: 10). On the other hand, it is intriguing (and again, perhaps, symptomatic of Fanon's distrust) that *Home of the Brave*, a mainstream Hollywood war film released in 1949, should be used to illustrate, and confirm, Fanon's sceptical approach to the uses and abuses of psychoanalysis in the United States. In the remainder of this chapter, I want to put *Home of the Brave* back into *Black Skin, White Masks*, to use the film to clarify not only what psychoanalysis means to Fanon, but how the themes of psychoanalysis, cinema and war can be brought together through his work.

It is well-documented that the history of psychoanalysis as both theory and practice is intimately bound up with the history of two world wars and, in particular, with the clinical treatment of the so-called combat neuroses. Whatever the combination of features attributed to them – amnesia, disturbed sleep, restlessness, fear, jerking limbs, dejection, depression, hysterical paralyses, recurrent nightmares, feelings of weakness and dizziness – the war neuroses, in the words of a 1944 *Newsweek* article, 'wrought strange changes in fighting men', undermining their 'mental peace and stability', and, perhaps more importantly, their ability to fight (29 May 1944: 68). Freud's theories of trauma and anxiety allowed army psychiatrists and doctors to answer the question: why did some men break down under combat and others not? The success of psychotherapeutic treatments in getting frontline 'nervous cases' 'to talk out their fears', as a 1943 issue of *Time* put it, led to psychoanalysis enjoying a considerable vogue in the 1940s (13 September 1943). Freud's notion of unconscious guilt proved, according to a 1944 article in the *New York Times*, that 'anybody could develop a psychoneurosis under certain circumstances', thus dismissing the then 'popular belief that "only weaklings" develop psychiatric disturbances' (17 May 1944: 36). In postwar America, the emphases in these popular writings on successful adaptation, on the healing effects of recall and catharsis of traumatic experiences, led to urgent calls for a new 'therapeutic activism' to combat the spread of mass neuroses amid war-fatigued American civilians (Golb 1987: 415). But if the impetus of war gave psychoanalytic psychiatry a boost, its optimistic vision of a universal cure for the discontents of American culture also tended to ignore what is, for Fanon, the *political* question for psychoanalysis: namely, its often unthinking echo of 'a pessimistic view of man', and its tendency, in therapeutic method, to unwittingly reproduce 'the free play of sado-masochistic myths' (Fanon cited in Taylor 1989: 29; Fanon and Tosquelles 1953: 364). These versions of psychoanalysis also ignore what, for him, was to become the crucial link between the *proper time and place* of individual psychoneuroses and the traumatic neuroses of culture.[4] In a moment, we shall see Fanon's own enraged response to this democratic rhetoric of cure and its demand that all of us are equally at risk, at war, with universal guilt-feelings; a rage (and a refusal) which he directs at the racial, postwar dreaming of Hollywood and, in particular, at *Home of the Brave*.

Produced by Stanley Kramer, one of Hollywood's most outspoken liberals, and directed by Mark Robson, *Home of the Brave* brought its exploration of the treatment of war neuroses into contact with the black experience of American racism. Risking a black lead, played by the war veteran James Edwards, the film was also part of a more general concern with psychoanalysis in the cinema of the 1940s in such films as John Huston's *Let There Be Light* (1946) and *Possessed* (1947). As Gabbard and Gabbard note in their *Psychiatry and the Cinema*, first published in 1987, the cathartic cure – or cure through the recall of forgotten, traumatic experience – is a central theme of *Home of the Brave*, one that provides its dramatic structure and climax in the acting out of repressed content. In this sense, the film both harks back to the origins of psychoanalysis – to Freud and Breuer's *Studies on Hysteria* published between 1893 and 1895 – and registers the postwar enthusiasm for the technique of narco-synthesis, which the *New York Times* compared to a 'mental x-ray' of anxieties buried deep in the 'subconscious' (17 May 1944: 36). Described by Nathan Hale as 'one of the most widely publicized treatments of the war neuroses', narcosynthesis derived from the clinical treatment of nervous breakdown during the Second World War (Hale 1995: 279). Combining the use of the barbiturate sodium penthothal and a highly directive psychotherapy, narcosynthesis was meant to stimulate the reliving of traumatic memories after the patient had been put into a 'synthetic dream state'. In 'War Neuroses', a pamphlet published in 1945, for example, John Grinker and Roy Spiegel advised that recovery from combat neurosis depended on the recall, and conscious reintegration, of battle experiences. The psychiatrist might play the part of a comrade lost, or wounded, in battle, or take the role of, as they put it, a 'reliable, but firm father figure', there to facilitate and to assuage the terror of recall (Grinker and Spiegel, cited in Hale 1995: 193).[5] The vividness of the recall often astonished the therapist, as the patient relived memories of combat. In severe cases, the results of penthothal were no less dramatic: the mute could talk; the deaf, hear; the paralysed, move; the terror-stricken, become calm. According to the *New York Times*, one of the most 'amazing revelations' of the method was the 'universality of guilt reactions' and, in many popular accounts of narcosynthesis, that guilt was taken back to early childhood experiences, buried deep in the unconscious mind (ibid.: 279). We are all guilty, according to this conventional parlance, and therefore all potentially curable. Thus narcosynthesis, or narcoanalysis as it was sometimes called, exemplified the idea that we can suffer from our memories, that we can be disabled by who we are – 'Your personality can literally kill you', warned the *Science Digest* in 1947 – at the same time as it set itself up as a psychodynamic cure for our unhappy lives.

It is against the background of this wider humanitarian interest in how psychoanalysis might cure 'our worst selves' – those selves mired in 'hate and murder', in the words of *Scientific American* – that the cathartic, and profoundly fantasmatic, machinery of cinema is set in motion. *Home of the Brave*, described as 'daring', presents a textbook case of the narcosynthetic treatment of a war neurosis which, simultaneously, delves into a lifetime's experience of racism. Part of a cycle of racial problem films appearing in 1949, *Home of the Brave*, along with *Pinky*, *Lost Boundaries*, and *Intruder in the Dust*, represents an exploration of anti-black racism coming out of Hollywood's 'wartime conscience-liberalism' (Cripps 1993: 221). The film tells the story of Peter Moss, a black American soldier, suffering from partial amnesia and an hysterical paralysis of the legs, who is coming to the end of his treatment by narcosynthesis. His army psychiatrist, played by Jeff Corey, is helping Moss to relive the experiences which, he believes, underlie the paralysis. In brief, Moss has witnessed the death of a lifelong friend, Finch, while on a map-making sortie to a Japanese-occupied Pacific island. Prior to Finch's death, they clash over the maps, a quarrel which ends with Finch calling Moss a 'yellow-bellied nigg ...'. He never completes the epithet because he is felled by a Japanese sniper's bullet. (The Japanese remain an invisible, profoundly alien, presence throughout the film. That difference, easily decodable in racial terms, marks out the black American patriot as someone who *belongs* to the nation, one of us, unlike the nation's enemy, the Japanese.) After the capture and torture of Finch by the Japanese, the four-man, racially integrated team is faced with the dilemma of going back for him or pressing on with their mission. As Finch's childhood friend, as well as comrade, the dilemma is carried by Moss. Just before his final cure, we see Moss alone on the beach of the island, babbling hysterically while cradling Finch, who has managed, despite being shot and tortured, to crawl back to the base camp. He dies in Moss's arms. As soon as he realises that his friend is dead, Moss discovers that he is paralysed. Against that backdrop, and in view of the flashbacks to Moss's childhood, the climax of the film returns to Moss lying on the psychiatrist's couch, under the influence of penthothal, being encouraged to recover the repressed sources of his 'bad feeling' while in a synthetic dream-state. What allows Moss to walk again, to speak his repressed hostility, is Finch's abusive epithet, but now mimed by the psychiatrist playing the role of racist aggressor. The film ends with Moss's cathartic cure – the release of his (self-punishing) racial hostility and anxiety – by the knowledge, relayed to him by a (now) crippled white soldier, that black soldiers, like whites, suffer from survivor guilt *in just the same way*. This emphasis on a shared humanity characterising Moss's feelings of hostility and relief toward his dead friend, however, also scotomises the role of racism in his breakdown. It forgets that other war so eloquently described by Fanon.

While the film's accomplishment was praised by white and black reviewers alike, others saw a confused portrayal of black humanity in Hollywood's depiction of racial harmony or integration, a confusion which *Home of the Brave* shared with those other racial 'problem' films. While purportedly about blacks, these films were also, as Ralph Ellison's 1949 review in *The Reporter* put it, 'not *about* Negroes at all; they are about what whites think and feel about Negroes' (Ellison 1949: 277). The black protagonists of these films are so unobtrusive and unthreatening, so virtuously self-effacing and morally upright, they can only be freely imagined as negroes in whiteface – in some instances, literally, as white actors played passing blacks in *Pinky* and *Lost Boundaries*. 'In varying degree', writes Ellison, 'these films were unwilling to dig into the grave to expose the culprit [a reference to the film, *Intruder in the Dust*], and thus we find them using ingenious devices for evading the full human rights of their Negroes' (ibid.: 278). One of those unexhumed 'culprits' was the issue of 'whether Negroes can rightfully be expected to risk their lives in an army in which they are slandered and discriminated against' (ibid.). Crucially, *Home of the Brave* can't seem to decide whether the war it portrays represents the daily struggle of blacks fighting against racism in military and civilian life, or the war between democracy and fascism, or both. While this should in no way be taken as a necessarily bad thing, for Ellison it signals a 'defeat not only of drama but of purpose' (ibid.). That 'purpose', in *Home of the Brave*, was not only to counter the widely held belief that Negroes make cowardly soldiers, but to answer the political, fascistic fantasy of black inferiority with the assimilationist fantasy of white liberalism. But the film's static image of American patriotism, and its repression of racism in favour of the universality of neurosis, could only offer the ingenious cure and consolation that blacks suffer in *the same* ways as whites. For blacks to be redeemed, then, freed from the traumas of racism, and welcomed back into the ties that bind nation and family, they must never be allowed to forget they are just *the same* as *us*; namely, white. While that cure may have produced a 'profuse flow of tears' and 'profound emotional catharsis' in white audiences, Ellison notes that it was met with 'derisive laughter' in predominantly Negro audiences (ibid.: 280).

That warring command or challenge – be the same but different – was implicit in the screenplay taken and adapted by Carl Foreman from Arthur Laurent's Broadway play of the same name. During its seasonal run on Broadway, *Home of the Brave* was commended for making a 'set of facts unbearably real' and for creating compelling drama out of a 'tale of inner and outer terror' (*Theatre Arts*, 30 March 1946: 141). In his screenplay, Foreman substituted a black GI for Laurent's Jewish protagonist, a move which many saw as the more radical option given the recent spate of films exploring anti-Semitism. It would be sadly ironic, then, if, in translating that liberal dream of integration from Jew to black, the screenplay forgot the ongoing lessons of Jim Crow segregation in the United States, a reality meaning vastly different things depending on whether you were black or Jewish. Foreman's screenplay avoided that tension by making his main protagonist a negro in whiteface. The screenplay, according to Cripps's *Making Movies Black* (1993), was the outcome of a compromise between the 'blatant propaganda' favoured by Foreman and Kramer's insistence on the notion that all men are 'the same' (Cripps 1993: 222). Instead of a working compromise in the filmic narrative, however, Ellison saw an '*evasion*', a 'sleight-of-hand', and one rooted in the film's inability to resolve American postwar anxieties about human rights and racial guilt through the ennobling dream of psychoanalysis – an insight strikingly contiguous with Fanon's, as we shall see (Ellison 1949: 278).

Home of the Brave charts Moss's progress from war to paralysis to therapy: the trajectory followed by any number of young men, black and white, during and after the Second World War. For at least one young black veteran watching this film, the experience is one of anger and paralysis transferred from screen to spectator. For Fanon, waiting to see himself on screen, waiting to see himself seen by the audience for the film, *Home of the Brave*, or *Je suis un nègre*, represents an 'amputation', advising the black spectator 'to adopt the humility of the cripple' (Fanon 1967: 140). 'The crippled veteran of the Pacific war', he explains, 'says to my brother, "Resign yourself to your colour the way I got used to my stump; we're both victims"' (ibid.). Fanon is referring to the closing scene of the film in which Moss, now cured, and Mingo, a fellow member of the mission now minus an arm (and wife), walk off together to open a bar and a restaurant. 'Coward', says Mingo in a powerful gesture of solidarity, 'take my coward's hand', a gesture which intricately intertwines their two histories in the 'equation'; 'a one-armed white man equals one whole Negro' (Cripps 1993: 224)[6] This, then, is the film's 'cure' for racism, its appeal to equality. That appeal refuses to equate civil justice with transgressed rights, substituting, instead, the commonality of a psychic wound which allows a black man to overcome his hysteria and debilitating internal war between guilt and duty. It is no wonder that Ralph Ellison identified an obsessive 'inner psychological need to view Negroes as less than men' in white America (Ellison 1949: 276). Or that Fanon should see the dominant motif of this film in the idea that blackness is an inhibiting factor which must be overcome if the personality is to return to the strength and mastery associated with whiteness; that Moss must resign himself to how his psychiatrist and Mingo see him: as a yellow-bellied nigger, or a cripple. That resignation, or the command to adapt yourself to the way in which the world sees you, may start to clarify Fanon's distrust of the application of so-called 'psychoanalysis' in American psychiatry and film. 'I am a master and I am advised to adopt the humility of a cripple', he continues. 'Yesterday, awakening to the world, I saw the sky turn upon itself utterly and wholly. I wanted to rise, but the disembowelled silence fell back upon me, its wings paralysed. Without responsibility, straddling Nothingness and Infinity, I began to weep' (Fanon 1967: 140).

This is a film, then, that made a grown man cry. Why? Why does this story of healing and cure choke, and paralyse, Fanon in his turn? Why does the film's melancholy spectacle open up an abyss for a spectator on the edge of some unlocatable, unreachable space spanning Nothingness and Infinity? It would be easy to say that Fanon weeps because he identifies with Moss, with a man who had a 'bad feeling' and doesn't know what it is, who is suffering from memories (both remembered and forgotten) of past injuries inflicted in the course of at least two wars: the race war and the world war. But it is worth noting, too, that Fanon saw the film some time between 1949 and 1951, while he was in Lyons, on a military scholarship, training as a psychiatrist. Like Moss, but differently, then, Fanon has gone from war to therapy to screen – and so to paralysis.

In one sense, *Home of the Brave*, like *Black Skin, White Masks*, is all about, is dedicated to overcoming, that paralysing split between being black and being human, being black and being white, being Martinican and being French – a split, finally, between conscious and unconscious formations of psychical and political identity. Fanon, like Moss, lived this war in himself, according to two temporalities or two analytical histories that were at the same time disjoined and inextricable. What is up there, waiting, for Fanon on screen is the image of a psychiatrist miming the role of racist aggressor – an image that, I want to suggest, has the potential to explode Fanon's psyche. Moss can't walk, and he doesn't know why; he has a 'bad feeling', and he doesn't know what it is. As the one who does know, the psychiatrist tells him that he can't walk because he does not want to and that his 'bad feeling' – one that Moss is inclined to explain in terms of his experience of racism – is just like everybody else's. The guilt he feels is just *the same* as every other soldier's. Every soldier feels glad that his friend, and not he, got the bullet; that triumph is an open secret: or, 'sensitivity is the disease you've got'. In other words, Moss, like Afro-Americans generally, is oppressed because he's sensitive, and sensitive because he's oppressed. *Home of the Brave* does not turn that 'sensitivity' into Moss's personal problem, but whatever its gesture towards the legacy of 150 years of slavery, and the postwar denial of black rights, the film inflects the cure as a simultaneously universalising and individualising process. 'That was it. That was the basic sameness – the strong will to live. ... That was the sameness' (cited in Miller 1949: 81). Moss is just like everybody else in that he shares a universal tendency to guilt; but, at the same time, the film suggests that 'to be really cured', he has to surmount a lifetime of racist persecution by those who believe he is different. Forget your blackness in the name of a shared humanity, then, but resign yourself to it as damage, disability, or 'stump'. Forget your blackness, but remember that you are, after all, a 'dirty nigger': remember, because your cure depends on it.

A full analysis of the film would have to make the connection between Finch's insult – 'You yellow-bellied nig ...' – and the doctor's taunts and coercive command, 'You dirty nigger, get up and walk!'. It would have to discover why, in its constant references to Moss as 'nigger', the film appears to insist on the very difference it works so hard to efface – as if the imago, the fantasy of blackness, that Fanon tracks throughout *Black Skin, White Masks* can be glimpsed behind the political radicalism officially endorsed. Such an analysis would also have to address the question of Jewishness in both screenplay and film.[7] But what I want to focus on here is the fact that, while on one level *Home of the Brave* wants to replace the black man's shame and guilt with legitimised anger, on another level, it cannot countenance the anger that such an endorsement might unleash. You did not wish Finch dead because he was white and you are black and he had insulted you, the doctor assures Moss. No, you were just glad to be alive. You did what you had to do as a soldier. In other words, even as it advises Moss, and its black spectators, to be angry rather than ashamed, *Home of the Brave* refuses to hear the black man's ambivalent expression of his anger at the insult hurled at him by his friend: 'I was glad he was dead'. With that refusal, the film misses, or dismisses, Moss's furious, and paralysing, encounter with the black imago apparent in his friend's speech: 'You yellow-bellied nig ...'. It makes that encounter secondary to another, and supposedly irreducible, human experience: the guilt of going to war and doing's one's duty and surviving a dying friend. Moreover, that dismissal is made possible, and reaffirmed by, the psychoanalytic cure. As Warren Miller puts it, in a contemporary review of the film: 'the psychiatrist is the means whereby the question raised [of the oppression of Negro people in America] is circumvented' (ibid.: 79).

'I refuse to accept that amputation' is Fanon's response to this albeit worthy attempt to defuse the aggression directed at, and then returned, guiltily, by the black man. For Fanon, that return is crucial because it opens onto the terrain of the black man's incessant war with himself. A war dominated by the dialectic of guilt and aggression, identification and refusal, being black and being white. It is not only that at this point in his life, Fanon is beginning to explore the dynamics of racist aggression and the 'vast black abyss' of black alienation through the language and concepts of psychoanalysis and existential phenomenology (Fanon 1967: 14). There is, I think, also something about the multiple identifications available to Fanon through *Home of the Brave* – the idealistic young volunteer, the black man struggling to come to terms with the experience of racism in both civilian and military life, the psychiatrist struggling to cure the internal war that paralyses the black body – something which shows up that screen for him as a conflict, a split in his own identity. 'But I am betrayed', Fanon concludes, in the course of a discussion of the absence of black archetypes in 'our' – European – literature. 'It's no good: I am a White Man. For, unconsciously, I guard against what is black in me, that is, the totality of my being' (ibid.: 191; t.m.); [*'Mais je suis trahi ... Rien a faire! je suis un Blanc. Or, inconsciemment, je me méfie de ce qui est noir en moi, c'est-à-dire, de la totalité de mon être'* [Fanon 1952: 154]]. As if troping the French title of *Home of the Brave* – *'Je suis un nègre'* – this is one of Fanon's most complex statements concerning the *identity* of the black man who is white and yet totally black. Reinflecting whiteness as distrust of (as being on guard against) blackness, Fanon then locates both being white and on guard, distrustful, in the unconscious: I am white because unconsciously I distrust what is black in me. That unconscious is not only 'on guard' and suspicious, it is partisan, embattled, like a garrison keeping watch over a conquered black ego. An ego coerced and condemned, not to freedom but to exile from its own desires, an ego abjectly incapable of transcendence: 'I am a negro – but naturally I do not know it, because I am one', Fanon writes, again evoking the French title of the film (t.m. 191); [*'je suis un nègre – mais naturellement je ne le sais pas, puisque je le suis'* [Fanon 1952: 155]]. In this sense, what Fanon is saying here starts to confound the logic of *Home of the Brave*, a film which wants to replace the consciousness – the 'sensitivity' – of being black with the unconsciousness of being white, that wants to forget blackness by making it white (though not quite). By contrast, for Fanon, blackness is already intruded upon, displaced by, an invasive whiteness which, as it were, gets there first; you cannot simply make black white because to be black is to be already, unconsciously, white. 'In the Antilles', Fanon suggests, 'perception always occurs on the level of the imaginary. It is in white terms that one perceives one's fellows' (1967: 163). That is, to be black is to be already interfered with, violated by, a whiteness which comes from the inside out. A whiteness that not only distrusts but hates.

But what do you do with an unconscious that appears to hate you? 'I had read it rightly', Fanon admits, commenting on Alan Burns' *Colour Prejudice*, published in 1948. 'It was hate; I was hated, detested, despised, not by the neighbour across the street or my cousin on my mother's side, but by an entire race. I was up against something unreasoned' (ibid.: 118; t.m.). That unreason, its hatred, is there, inside. But how do you make the black man's unconscious match his being, how do you make it black? You might write *Black*

Skin, White Masks: as part of a broader literary process committed to helping the collective, the community, move towards reflection, mediation. Fanon's reference here is arguably Sartre's decisive *What is Literature?*, a text fuelled by the pursuit of literary responsibility and decision, and one to which I will return towards the end of this chapter. 'This work', Fanon hopes, 'would be a mirror with a progressive infrastructure, in which the negro could (re)find himself on the road to disalienation' (ibid.: 184; t.m.). You might, as Fanon sometimes seems to do, deny that the black man has an unconscious – at least so far as the dynamics of racism are concerned. 'The racial drama being played out in the open', Fanon reasons, 'the Black Man does not have time "to make it unconscious"' (ibid.: 150); [*'Le drame racial se déroulant en plein air, le Noir n'a pas le temps to l'inconscienciser"'* 1952: 22].

Or you might speculate about the mechanism of intrusion, about how the black man is already split, preoccupied, by a racist, a conscious-unconscious, imago. The pain and anger unleashed by that imago introduces a new dynamic into the structure of identity, the self's desire to hurt the imago – that is, part of the self – in a passionate bid to escape it. There is an overwhelming lack of clarity about what intrusion means for Fanon when it comes to the black self or ego. The term conveys a complex array of images, 'intrusion' being variously defined as the real and imaginary irruption of a racial counterpart (of *'l'imago du semblable'*), an irruption synonymous with the experience of being invaded and breached by the 'unidentifiable and unassimilable' (1967: 161). To understand this idea of an ego literally enveloped by an affective, specular suggestion, it is necessary to look at how Fanon reads the psychodynamics of that intrusion – its affective organisation and registration of the real world – in strictly racial terms: intrusion, for Fanon, is indissociable from racialised disparagement and anxiety, a transformation of his source for the term, Lacan's 1938 *Encyclopédie française* article, *'Les complexes familiaux'*. In fact, the psychoanalytic formula for the cultural origins of intrusion comes straight out of Lacan's concept of the *imago*, but with one important difference. While, for Lacan, the state of intrusion includes 'delusional beliefs' which he traces to the first alienation of desire begun in an *imaginary* identification, or *méconnaisance*, the unassimilable elements of those beliefs have no racial markers. What gets eliminated in this version, therefore, is any facticity, or racial corporeality of the body. In Fanon's reading, however, there is no doubt about it: the aggressivity directed at the racial imago of the other derives from the subject's own internal aggressivity which, in its attempts to flee the traumas of the visible, the imaginary, latches onto introjected, negrophobic elements from culture. Here, the wincing bridle of intrusion reveals how black identity has been infiltrated by a racially specific social dialectic.

> It would certainly be interesting, using the Lacanian notion of the *mirror stage*, to ask to what extent the *imago* of his counterpart (*semblable*) built up in the white youngster at the usual age would suffer an imaginary aggression at the appearance (*apparition*) of the Black Man (*du Noir*). When the process described by Lacan is understood, there can be no more doubt that the true Other of the White Man (*Autrui du Blanc*) is and remains the Black man (*le Noir*). And vice versa. (1967: 61, 131, t.m.)[8]

This culturalisation of Lacan's *le stade du miroir* as well as his account of the ego's *imaginary* genesis is complicated, but Fanon could not be more clear. The ego may well be captured and retrieved by an imaginary unity through a reflected body image, bound to primitive libidinal drives – a capture which Lacan argued was 'inscribed in imaginary tensions, like all other libidinal tensions. Libido and ego are on the same side' – but for Fanon, that imaginary front of the ego can also be injected by the hatreds and anxieties of culture (Lacan 1988a: 26). Indeed, rather than stemming from a general ontology of 'misrecognition', the historic lineage of that specular structure in the Antilles begins with colonial hegemony and racism. This was evident. Like a garrison keeping watch over a conquered city, the mechanism of intrusion suggests that there is no gap between the spectacle or stadia of a military occupation, and those quasi-internal wars of the black psyche: 'the true Other of the White Man is and remains the Black man'. Already possessed by colonialism's total war, the imago of the black is just another battle front in the manichean conflict between coloniser and colonised. The battle lines are drawn over the imago of blacks, and Fanon turns to the psychoanalytic concept of phobia to think that aggression – its possibility – so as to cure and acquit the pathogenic nature of its repulsions and fears: 'The choice of the phobic object', he writes, 'is … *overdetermined*. This object does not come at random out of the void of nothingness … it is enough that somewhere it *exist*: It is a possibility' (1967: 55).

We are back with the black man's war with himself, with his waiting – 'If I were asked for a definition of myself', Fanon reminds us, 'I would say that I am one who waits' (ibid.: 120) – for an imago that is already there, lying in wait for him. It's a moment of suspension, one that delays, perhaps permanently, the timely expression of anything that might be called one's own. It is as if the black is permanently belated, as if he becomes suddenly aware of an unconscious running all by itself. At the same time as he distrusts it, Fanon is forced back to psychoanalysis: 'I am willing to work on the psychoanalytic level – in other words, the level of the "failures", in the sense in which one speaks of engine failures' (ibid.: 123). In so far as a black imago – a white, and distrusting, unconscious – comes to dominate, or inhabit, the black psyche, the desire to offset the anxiety resulting from this intrusion leads to the transferral of negrophobic fantasies – experienced by blacks and whites – onto other blacks. And it is precisely this transference that takes Fanon back to the Antilles, to those fantasists who, on the level of the imaginary at least, appear to dream themselves white.

'[I]n the Antilles', Fanon writes, 'perception always occurs on the level of the imaginary. It is in white terms that one perceives one's fellows' (ibid.: 163). That somatic delusion discloses a clash of cultures as well as an intolerable impasse. French colonial 'imposition', interrupting the royal road of these dreams, has trapped them at the level of the imaginary. That occupation reemerges in what Fanon calls the neurotic abnormalities of Martinican family life. In Martinican family and cultural life, Fanon sees an ambivalence boosted by a 'masochistic' dedication to the culture of mainland France, much of it no doubt provoked by a mimetic overidentification with a French family romance.[9] Imprinted on and imitated, in turn, by children already seduced by the allures and promises of that worship, Martinican culture is, for Fanon, at the mercy of a sacrificial superego whose 'abnormality' leaves its mark in the form of somatic delusions, confusional anxieties and hypochondriacal panic. I have already touched on these arguments in my brief discussion of Fanon in Chapter 1. As Fanon contends in his chapter on 'The Negro and Psychopathology', the black child's identification with the stories and images of white culture leads to a direct correlation between the imago of blacks in cultural life and black self-images. Here, the dreamwork of the black child (and adult) designates a psychic elision or caesura at the intersection of the imago, the stereotype and the ego's *mise-en-scène*, an elision disclosing an embarrassing conformity to French racism, a dreamwork which can only establish ties to the outside world by re-projecting itself as white.

Fanon is scathing in his dismissal of this cultural sickness, contemptuous of the psychic and political paralysis emerging from this 'sacrificial dedication' to French racial hegemony and colonial imposition (ibid.: 147). Everywhere he looks he sees the nihilistic débris of a persecutory degradation, in every face the localised radiance of dreams shaded by the 'abnormal' bonds of phobia (ibid.: 152). Turning to Nietzsche, he sees in this '*ressentiment*' the expedient 'reaction' of a slave-culture unwilling to discharge itself from an irredeemable psychic debt; a culture unwilling to wake from the nightmare of its history (ibid.: 222). Antilleans were lost, then, both to themselves and to each other. Having 'devoured' what they projected onto the white world, they were doomed to be consumed by these very same projections from French racist culture. If they dreamed of a long overdue family reunion with their descendants, the Gauls, that was because, unconsciously, they had already disavowed the fact that the old injustices continued to persist, that, for many of the French, they could only be 'good niggers'. Further, they lived in fear of what they had denied, overwhelmed by the permanently black tain of the mirror. Quick to deny any kinship – any connection – with the Senegalese, or black Africa, they split blackness into a true and an improper destiny, or designation. Trying to bring that delusional fear into sharper definition, Fanon turns away from the idea of repressed, pathogenic scenes or desires, to the 'closed' world of colonial society (ibid.: 143). It is easily forgotten, he writes, citing René Ménil, the Martinican poet and philosopher, how, in Martinique, '*the establishment, in place of the repressed spirit, of the representative authority of the master in slave consciousness*', 'an authority instituted at the heart of the collectivity', is solely there to keep watch over black identities 'as a garrison does over a conquered city' (Ménil 1996: 131). Only in the conquered city of Fort-de-France could the vanquished seek to erase their inconsolable shame by becoming a mimed travesty of their victors.

Beyond any doubt, Fanon sees rancour in this enchanted rapture, as well as a certain filial subservience to, or legacy from, *la mère patrie*. The Antillean who dreams and hopes of a complete assimilation to the mother-country (or of being Tarzan) is, for Fanon, already dreaming white dreams which are, in turn, projected onto another black war machine, the Senegalese. That dreaming had, he writes, also been his own years before he dreamt of joining up with General de Gaulle, the great white father. 'As a schoolboy', he tells us, 'I had many occasions to spend whole hours talking about the supposed customs of the savage Senegalese', a way of thinking, of talking about, the Senegalese that is 'essentially white' (1967: 148). For Fanon, this recollection demonstrates the alienation of the young Antillean – himself – from his blackness, a crystallisation of an attitude through which the black Antillean learns to transfer onto the Senegalese the horror, and the fascination, that the white feels for him. A little later, we learn that Fanon was thirteen when, for the first time, he saw Senegalese soldiers, a sight preceded, he tells us, by years of lurid anecdotes about *'la force noire'*: *le tirailler sénégalais*.[10]

> All I knew about them was what I heard from veterans of the First World War: 'They attack with the bayonet, and, when that doesn't work, they just punch their way through the machine-gun fire with their fists. ... They cut off "heads" and collect human ears'.

'These Senegalese were in transit from Martinique, on their way from Guiana', he continues,

> I scoured the streets eagerly for a sight of their uniforms, which had been described to me: red fezzes and belts. My father went to the trouble of collecting two of them, whom he brought home and who had the family in raptures. It was the same thing in school. My mathematics teacher, a lieutenant in the reserve who had been in command of a unit of Senegalese troopers in 1914, used to make us shiver with anecdotes: 'When they are praying they must never be disturbed, because then the officers cease to exist. They're lions in battle, but you have to respect their customs'. (ibid.: 162–3)

The African Muslim is savage and fearless, *'d'un bon garçon simplet mais brave'*: and the blacker he is, the more savage he is, that is, if you are an Antillean, or a black Frenchmen (Garrigues 1991: 42). As a schoolboy, Fanon bore witness to this savagery second-hand; he already knew what these signs and symbols meant: those uniforms, those red fezzes and belts, in their rapturous and fearful significance, involve a desire to see and to know, or see confirmed at any rate, a truly black alterity, an aboriginal force prepared to die in war for *Madame la France*. Throughout *Black Skin, White Masks*, Fanon's references to the Senegalese repeat this structure of rapt spectatorship, of fearful pleasure. That myth of the courageous *tirailleur*, powerfully perpetuated in the deepest of Antillean social divisions, allows Fanon to interrogate Antillean 'masochism' through the figure of a black *Übermensch* as seen through the hallucinosis of Antillean dreams. If those truly black soldiers provide a dream, or nightmare, of a racial kinship which cannot be acknowledged as such, Fanon sees another conquest and exclusion inhabiting that fear. In this debacle of Martinicans beside themselves with excitement, celebrating a military review of French colonial might, he sees every evidence of a neurotic 'erethism' (Fanon 1967: 152). As war machines cutting off human heads and collecting human ears, as fanatics unaware of their own fanaticism whose loyalty and patriotism are admired throughout the Empire, the Senegalese can themselves be collected, by the father, by the young Fanon, as a metonym of the absolute other already within the self; an Other whose mechanical, involuntary affect – shivers, raptures – can never be appeased, only deferred. For the Antilleans who come to see them, then, the Senegalese continue to signify an absolute break between racial identity and cultural heritage, phylogenetic memory and racial phenotype.

It is no coincidence that Fanon should draw attention to this Antillean image of the Senegalese as all that is inassimilable, socially undesirable and unacceptable, while also fervently – exotically – admired. It is the utter blackness of the Senegalese which allows the Antilleans to dream of a whiter being. But, as we have already seen, this fantasy is itself troubled by another war – the aggression, and hatred, of French cultural life directed at *all* blacks, a war which gives the lie to the belief: *'Avant, j'étais nègre, maintenant, je suis français'* ('Before, I was a negro; now I am French'). It would take the racist, Vichy occupation of Admiral Robert to destroy this imaginary whitening by introducing Martinicans to the war of the real. It is at this point, I think, that we can return, with Fanon, to Vichy occupied Martinique. In the essay, 'Antilleans and Africans', published in *Towards the African Revolution*, Fanon, lingering on the question of war and delusion, argues that the occupation brought to an end these dreams of proper and improper racial being. It did so by arriving as a limit, or ontological force, on the royal road of the Antillean dream: the white sailors of the *Béarn* and the *Émile-Bertain* proceeded to fascistically rename the devotion and allegiance of black Martinicans to the France of Maréchal Petain.[11] Destroying that romance of an inseparable union between Martinique and France, these Vichy occupying forces also brought home to the Antilleans the distressing scene of their own abjection, now openly named and shamed as utterly *nègre*. It was a devastating revelation, undermining, in one moment, the political imaginary of the Antilles. Here, again, war provides the means of traumatic paralysis, especially for the black, who, as we discovered earlier, is petrified by this revelation. Fanon, of course, already knew this would be the case because he himself was white-identified; an identity effectively obliterated by his encounters with the shaming exclusion – or rejection – of French and Nazi racism, but also reconstituted by his journey from paralysis to therapy. The question is, what did this revelation reveal to him, about to enter into the war, and later, psychiatry? And what dialectical notion of the cure did he derive from this *prise de conscience*?

Black Skin, White Masks has a particular way of imagining *la guerre noire*, that psychic, quasi-internal war of the black man battling with himself; that 'struggle for existence' which Ralph Ellison, in a 1942 article on the war, 'The Way It Is', said 'constitutes a war in itself' (Ellison 1967: 291). Part of that imagining owes much, of course, to the voyeuristic condescensions of Hollywood cinema – condescensions to which I want, briefly, to return. We already know that Fanon was profoundly dissatisfied with the last scene of *Home of the Brave* and its crippling appeal to a shared disfigurement. Moss, we are told, did what he had to do. That he was no 'different' from any other white soldier, either in his fear of death or in his intense sense of guilt. That he was, after all, human in obeying a more primordial sense of duty to himself: the duty of self-preservation. And yet, in that final fraternal scene with Mingo, the choices open to him – paralysis or amputation – are aporetic because they already attest to his having been invaded by a foreign force, by conflicting imperatives. That figure of aporia, and the lesson it imparts on how blacks are 'condemned' to freedom, makes a powerful resurgence in Fanon's reimagining of the links between black existential literature and psychoanalysis.

I would like to explore the suggestion that at least part of Fanon's refusal of the moral aporia, or law, facing the black soldier in *Home of the Brave*, comes to him by way of literature, more specifically Jean-Paul Sartre's definition of 'committed' literature in *What is Literature?*: *littérature engagée*. An account of *Black Skin, White Masks* as 'literature' – the Sartrean idea of literature which it annexes – may well be central to the warring intelligibility and style of Fanon's work. Defining literature's 'really *contemporary* task' as the need 'to persuade the group to progress to reflection and mediation', Fanon reaffirms that task in his turn to Richard Wright's *Native Son* and Sartre's 1947 play, *La Putain respectueuse*, two texts which Fanon will draw on to analyse how, according to Wright, the 'whole inner landscape of American Negro life' is driven by a 'tremendous fund' of guilt and 'repression' (Wright 1946: xxx). The first reference to *Home of the Brave* in *Black Skin, White Masks* appears, notably enough, as a footnote to these reflections. In any event, Fanon's notion of a black man petrified into 'nonexistence' by a look comes by way of a detour, a description, of black guilt and fear as seen through *La Putain respectueuse* and *Native Son* (Fanon 1967: 139). In Wright's text, according to Fanon, 'it becomes possible for him [the Negro] to work off his aggression' (ibid.: 184). Part of that aggression is the reaction, by black men, to the open hatred of the democracies they were being asked to die for, a conflict which soon leads to another: a black man at war with himself, locked in inexorable combat between a desire for 'transcendence' and moral self-abnegation. 'Moral consciousness', Fanon writes, 'implies a kind of scission, a fracture of consciousness into a bright part and an opposing black part. In order to achieve morality, it is essential that the black, the dark, the Negro vanish from consciousness. Hence a Negro is forever in combat with his own image' (ibid.: 194). Turning to Wright and Sartre to explore that combat, Fanon also turns to the idea of committed literature to underscore his distrust of how psychoanalysis is 'applied' in the sickness of a postwar world fractured by this '*real* reality of our time' – colonial racism (Wright 1946: xxiv).

If this has any validity, then the aggressions and coercions of culture already cross, for Fanon, the frontier between literature and war. Yet, how does Fanon *think* that frontier? First, he mines the picture of black guilt and fear appearing in *Native Son* for the light it casts on the moral aporia condemning the black man to a 'feeling of nonexistence'. 'Sin is negro as virtue is white', he writes, confessing: 'I am guilty. I do not know of what, but I feel that I am a wretch [*un misérable*]' (Fanon 1967: 139, t.m.). That feeling, although conspicuously enigmatic is also disturbingly real, deeply enmeshing the moral self in nausea, paralysis, a shaming *réaction originelle* (Sartre 1969: 291). At the same time, that battleground is fraught with anxiety about the kind of summary judgement one is likely to receive from the white world, here making an entrance through the figure of whites holding guns – a figure of injustice so dismally implicated in a history of violence and power, it is hard to imagine a more unethical provenance. Second, Fanon uses *Native Son* as an illustration of black angst, as an example of a self stricken and overrun by anxieties blocking the subject from any sense of moral community:

> It's Bigger Thomas – who's afraid, terribly afraid. He is afraid, but of what is he afraid? Of himself. No one knows yet who he is, but he knows that fear will occupy the world when the world finds out. And when the world knows, the world expects something of the negro. He is afraid lest the world know, he is afraid of the fear

> that the world would feel if the world knew. Like that old woman on her knees who begged me to tie her to her bed.
>
> 'I just know, Doctor: Any minute that thing will take hold of me'.
>
> 'What thing?'
>
> 'The wanting to kill myself. Tie me down, I'm afraid'.
>
> In the end, Bigger Thomas acts. To put an end to the tension, he acts, he comes up to the world's anticipation. (Fanon 1967: 139, t.m.)

Existence might be a daily struggle for us all, but for the black his being is the *effect* of a war fought on at least two fronts. He must enter into combat not only with the presentiments and premonitions of a world condemning him to nonexistence, he must also enter the lists against his own image. That battle, though principally conceived in grand metaphysical terms as an Hegelian war over 'reciprocal recognitions', an ontological war in which existence 'is always a question of annihilation or triumph', is also a tenacious street war over the simple right to live (ibid.: 218, 228). That war, or wars, results in an irredeemable and massively expansive web of affect, verging on an imaginary, profoundly missed encounter with the 'thing' that one detests, that is the object of one's relentless dread, the thing that is oneself. Or, as Bigger's lawyer says in court:

> Every movement of his body is an unconscious protest. Every desire, every dream, no matter how intimate or personal, is a plot for conspiracy. Every hope is a plan for insurrection. Every glance of the eye is a threat. *His very existence is a crime against the state!* (Wright 1983: 434).[12]

This image of an unconscious protest against the psychic *state* – the fantasy – of what it means to be black is, for Fanon, already violent, already conceptually, even empirically, a sure sign that Bigger has reached the state of perpetual war, a total war without mediation or redress. Trapped on the frontier between Nothingness and Infinity, being and existence, living life 'on the outside of the world peeping in through a knot-hole in the fence' the black can only struggle against unwinnable odds (ibid.: 58).

Yet, again, this suspended entry repeats a more generalised foreclosure, or ethical impasse. Contrary to the condemnation by the interdictory, always violent, imperatives of cultural life, a violence inseparable from the 'anticipation' at the seat of Bigger's anxiety, Fanon turns to the *necessity*, 'the possible impossibility', of freedom

(Fanon 1967: 218, t.m.). 'My black skin', Fanon writes towards the end of *Black Skin, White Masks*, 'is not the depository of specific values. A long time ago, the starry sky that left Kant panting for breath delivered its secrets to us. And the moral law is doubtful of itself' (ibid.: 227). It is important to note that Fanon is not denying Kant's confidence in the sublime presentation of moral ideas which, in the *Critique of Judgement*, Kant argues discloses the whole power (*Macht*) of the mind. Rather he is stating that Kant's enthusiasm for the infinitude of the starry heavens – the infinitude which allows us to recognise, in turn, the infinite destiny of our own moral nature – must be retrieved in the Antilles. It must happen, there, because of the racial distribution of guilt and its paralysis at the level of the imaginary. In short, these Antilleans have been unable to locate the sublime infinity and authority of moral law within themselves precisely because colonial racism imposes on them, through the notion of duty or patriotic loyalty, an impossible demand which can never be satisfied justly: be like me and do not be like me, be white but not quite. Colonial war reveals the limits of Kant's fantasy of distributive justice in its perpetual readiness to wage war against the colonised at the level of both ideological fantasy and psyche. The moral law is no longer certain of itself in the Antilles not, or not only, because of the interdependency between law and hysterical violence, but because of the way in which colonialism has introduced a traumatic kernel, or aporia, into those Antilleans already at war with themselves. We've already seen why this imaginary paralysis interrupts both the time of analysis and of duty. *Black Skin, White Masks* explores this aporia in terms of a *political* question: namely, what is it about colonial authority that allows it to generate forms of inner unreason at the level of agency rather than Kant's inner freedom of moral law? What is it about the autonomous imposition of duty in a racially unjust society that turns the black subject into a peculiarly abject, masochistic obscenity?

In *Black Skin, White Masks*, these questions flank a double divide between war and film, war and literature. Nor should we forget the line that divides and separates Fanon's interest in psychoanalysis. If he declined the applications of American psychoanalysis as seen on film, Fanon nonetheless returns to the issue of cure and therapy through the redoubtable witnessing of Afro-American literature. My suggestion is that, despite being fiction, Fanon read *Native Son* for its powerful clinical insights into the psychopathologies of black men, and, by extension, for its existential formulations on the relation between cultural violence and the black psyche at war.[13] From hysterical paralysis to the quasi-military effractions of intrusion, from film to literature, the reverberations of war echo throughout *Black Skin, White Masks*. A major force in the national visions shaping postwar democracies, that war, or wars, not only confounds Fanon's vision of himself; it also forces him to rethink, in racial terms, the meaning of freedom, justice, and morality. It was this *political* resistance that led him to challenge the role of racist imagoes and their reproduction of the black ego as already breached – violated – by culture. And it was through the question of war that Fanon, for better or worse, arrived at his most troubling insights into the unconscious conflicts of black identity. The repercussive histories of that war also crossed the frontiers of psychoanalysis and philosophy. It is the force and challenge of Fanon's thinking that he works at that juncture of war, philosophy and psychoanalysis to leave us with a question: what do you do with an unconscious which appears to hate you?

Notes

1. Parts of this chapter were first given as lectures at the conference 'Frantz Fanon's *Black Skin, White Masks*', Institute of Romance Studies, University of London, 1997 and at the Center for Twentieth Century Studies, University of Wisconsin-Milwaukee, 1997. My special thanks to Roland Francois-Lack and Christopher Lane for inviting me to take part, and to Herbert Blau, Jane Gallop, Kathleen Woodward, Vicky Lebeau and Michael Temple for their comments and criticisms.
2. Those conflicts, as we shall see, also speak to an acute crisis in the family romance of *les Antilles* following the defeat of France in 1940 and the three years of traumatic occupation by the pro-Vichyist military regime; an occupation which Fanon was to later describe as the colonies' 'first metaphysical, or if one prefers, ontological experience' (Fanon 1970: 34). I shall be returning to Fanon's thought on this rupture towards the end of this chapter.
3. There are any number of junctures in Fanon's enigmatic, often unstable, essays and books where war, conflict, is signaled by a concern with *mediation* in both analysis and philosophy. While he has been accused, for example, of being too Hegelian in his assumptions, too fond of a concept of authentic liberation, Fanon's concern with *freedom* in both psyche and culture is nonetheless a haunted one: shrouded by abyssal insecurities and negativities; inhabited by an experience of finitude and decision going way beyond the simple, existential oppositions of the manichean into a teleological suspension of the ethical. Colonial war or military occupation, for example, so overwhelms the identity of the colonised with a 'defect' that 'inter-

dicts all ontological explication', decolonisation can only be boosted by an absolute '*tabula rasa*', a perilous, empty cataclysm, without origin or foundation, at one remove from either a representational politics of the subject or a politics of representation (Fanon 1967: 109; 1967a: 27). *At the same time*, that war or 'defect' is also being played out in the repetitions and affects of the transference of which Fanon was well aware in his analyses of his traumatised patients. Now, it is precisely in this tabula rasa without borders or frontiers and those psyches dispossessed by war and occupation, that all Fanon's interpretive decisions were taken and his analytical responsibilities begin. A univocal interpretation (be it dramaturgical, existential, political, or psychoanalytic) can never formalise these decisions and responsibilities totally, still less master their contents. Recent attempts to forge a more interdisciplinary approach to Fanon's work by Taylor (1989) and by Hall (1996) are thus to be welcomed.

4. In a dispute with Octave Mannoni over the latter's interpretation of the links between dreams and cultural trauma, Fanon called into question Freud's theory of the dreamwork. Rather than opening onto the royal road of the unconscious, Fanon saw dreams and the whole spectacle of colonial psychic relations as already marked by the real, by 'real fantasies', by the *scene* of cultural stereotypes. Indeed, it could be argued that he extended this insight to racial psychopathology in general. For example, in *Black Skin, White Masks*, he writes:

   > A few years ago, I remarked to some friends during a discussion that in a general sense the white man behaves towards the Negro as an elder brother reacts to the birth of a younger. I have since learned that Richard Sterba arrived at the same conclusion in America. (ibid.: 157)

   Sterba's article, 'Some Psychological Factors in Negro Race Hatred and Anti-Negro Riots', first published in 1947, analyses the unconscious motives of white analysands who participated in, or who were affected by, Detroit's race riots of June 1943. In his discussion of these analysands' dreams, Sterba, following Freudian theory, suggested that racial phobias derive from repressed sibling rivalry. Playing the role of an imaginary, younger sibling in these unconscious fantasies, Negroes were represented as 'unwelcome intruders' (Sterba 1947: 412). The imprint of culture on the dreamwork, or of dreamwork on culture, to be sure, allowed these analysands to satisfy their destructive drives through a substitute object – the Negroes who happened to be out on the streets during the actual riots (men mostly). Sterba discerned in the analysands' dreams repeated attempts to offset oedipal anxieties: apparently, they could satisfy their repressed hatred of the white father only by the real and symbolic murder of black men. Such displacements allowed positive feelings for the father to remain intact, while ambivalent emotional ties to the father were allowed to appear – as a cultural and unconscious fantasy of racial intrusion – through substitute objects. These time-honoured – and typical – dreams may have been inexorably compelling for the rioters, but what did the black men suffering real injury because of these oedipal ties make of this desire, which tried to sacrifice them to protect the prestige of the white father? Put slightly differently, did the fraternal role these black imagoes performed allow the desire for real racial murder on the outside to intrude on these dreams of paternal hatred, and in a way that is not simply described as an example of the real becoming fantasy? Could not these dreams – in becoming real – reveal the fixations where culture and unconscious fantasy become inseparable? A place also marked by the eruption of unconscious hatred into the real and, conversely, by the breaking in of a murderous real into the white (and black) unconscious? For a reading of Fanon's concept of 'real fantasies' see Vicky Lebeau's superb 'Psycho-politics: Frantz Fanon's *Black Skin, White Masks*' in J. Campbell and J. Harbord (eds), *Psycho-politics and Cultural Desires* (1998), London: Taylor and Francis.

5. Critics of narcosynthesis questioned whether the recall was a recovery and synthesis of a forgotten memory or an intensely animated miming out of the traumatic event under the direction of the therapist. If the latter, then the recalled memories were adjudged to be 'fictional' or 'highly distorted'. Such questions – on whether the method encourged a miming of affect – raises wider issues beyond the scope of this chapter. For a consideration of the treatment of combat neuroses in relation to whether the emotional acting out of the trauma in the sedated (or trance) state occurs in a profound absence from, or forgetfulness of the self; or, whether in this state of cathartic repetition it is not affective representations that are being remembered but the acting out of a state of dissociation in which the patient suffers beyond himself, beyond memory and self-representation, see Ruth Leys 'Traumatic Cures: Shell Shock, Janet, and the Question of Memory', *Critical Inquiry* 20 (Summer, 1994): 623–62.
6. By the same token, as James Baldwin, reviewing the film in *The Devil Finds Work* (1976), points out: 'why is the price of what should, after all, be a simple human connection so high? Is it really necessary to lose a woman, an arm, or one's mind, in order to say hello?' (*Collected Essays*, Library of America, 1998: 529). Baldwin's sceptical, dismissive response to *Home of the Brave* stems from its homosocial alignment with 'the American legend of masculinity' in which 'a black man and a white man can come together only in the absence of women' (ibid.).
7. I hope to address both issues in a later project.
8. For an excellent reading of Fanon's 'appropriation' of Lacan, see Stuart

Hall, 'The After-Life of Frantz Fanon', in Alan Read (ed.), *The Fact of Blackness* (London: ICA, 1996): 26–7.

9. See Richard D. E. Burton's *Il est l'auteur de La famille coloniale. La Martinique et la Mère-Patrie 1789–1992* (Paris: L'Harmattan, 1994).
10. For the imperialist rhetoric of *'la force noire'*, see Lieutenant-colonel Mangin, *La Force noire*, Paris: Hachette, 1910; and M. Michel, *L'Appel à l'Afrique. Contributions et réactions à l'effort de guerre en A. O. F., 1914–1919*, Paris: Publications de la Sorbonne, 1982.
11. For a commentary on this episode see Richard D. E. Burton's 'Vichyisme et vichyistes à la Martinique', in *Cahiers du CERAG* 34 (1978).
12. Wright's recourse to the topic of law in a novel exploring prohibition and paralysis raises some intriguing questions about the relation between black anxiety and law, questions which I cannot pursue here. Suffice it to say, Wright's concern with the visibility of black crime over and against the invisibility of black existence, raises some interesting points of comparison to Fanon's concerns with exhibition, image, dread, nonexistence.
13. But from the other direction, Wright, with great representational and intellectual force in *Native Son*, also saw a direct, radical correlation between psychoanalysis, psychiatry and literature. In his 1940 essay, 'How Bigger Was Born', Wright describes how, in his attempt to peer 'into the dim reaches of his incommunicable life' and the 'dim negative' of Bigger's character – an attempt resonating closely with a desire to overcome his own 'mental censor' – he turns to the 'unconscious, or pre-conscious, assumptions and ideals upon which nations and races act and live' (Wright 1983: 10, 20, 24, 21). His insights into those images and ideals, as set out in his 1946 'Introduction' to *Black Metropolis*, lead him to argue for an analytical interpretation of the sublimatory force of black 'personality mechanisms' which he saw as militating against more radical solutions to black 'racial resentments' built-up during the war. The same year he helped co-found, with his one-time analyst and lifelong friend, the psychiatrist, Frederic Wertham, the first racially integrated free psychiatric clinic in New York – the Lafargue Psychiatric Clinic in Harlem. That clinic, described by Ralph Ellison as 'perhaps the most successful attempt in the nation to provide psychotherapy for the underprivileged', bore a striking parallel to Fanon's postwar developments in analytical sociotherapy (Ellison 1948: 294–5; Bulhan 1985). While this comparison needs a much fuller analysis than I am prepared to give it here, in his essay 'Harlem is Nowhere', first written in 1948, Ellison describes the most immediate impact of the clinic as an 'extension of democracy' in its forthright and 'scientific willingness to dispense with preconceived notions and accept the realities of the Negro' (Ellison 1948: 295, 301). The ineffable demands of treating the 'obscene absurdity' of those

realities which, in Harlem, 'are indistinguishable from the distorted images that appear in dreams', for Ellison and for Wright lay in finding a cure for the 'sickness of the social order' (ibid.: 296, 298, 302). 'Not quite citizens and yet Americans', 'Negroes', Ellison observes, 'are not unaware that the conditions of their lives demand new definitions of terms like *primitive* and *modern, ethical* and *unethical, moral* and *immoral, patriotism* and *treason, tragedy* and *comedy, sanity* and *insanity*' (ibid.: 297–8). Arguably, this was precisely the 'anasemic' rhetoric Fanon was looking for when he wrote *Black Skin, White Masks* while evolving the techniques of his sociotherapy. It is not therefore surprising, given this shared, passionate desire to use psychiatric insights 'to reforge the will to endure in a hostile world', that Fanon, Wright and Ellison should seek a discourse of emancipation outside the closed borders and debilitating psychodramas of traditional psychiatry (Ellison 1967: 302).

V Father Stories

> The rule is that there are no good fathers; it is not the men that are at fault, but the paternal bond that is rotten. (Jean-Paul Sartre, *Les Mots*)

'Narrating', as Peter Brooks has said, 'is never innocent' (Brooks 1984: 77). Father stories, according to John Edgar Wideman, are also never safe: 'A MOTHERFUCKER AIN'T IT. THIS DADDY SEARCH' (Wideman 1994: 77). Searching for his father, and his father's fathers, through his powerful memoir, *Fatheralong*, first published in 1994, Wideman describes that daddy search as a 'trope, a ropa-dope trope containing enough rope to hang you up terminally' (ibid.: 77). To hang you up? To hang a black son in the name of the father? The risk, or gamble, of retelling black father stories is clearly extreme for Wideman, driving him to uncover the threat of a lynching embedded in his potentially terminal (motherfucking?) quest for his father. But the stakes of that quest are high. Concluding his memoir with a critique of how the paradigms of racism continue to come between 'my grandfathers and myself, my father and me', Wideman wants *Fatheralong* to act as a counter to America's 'tradition of obscuring, stealing, or distorting black people's lives' (ibid.: 197, 196). That tradition of theft and distortion (and, I would add, of lynching) is the starting-point for Wideman's attempt to give voice to 'me', 'my', 'us', to reclaim the father by getting the father to reclaim the son – and so start to resolve a dilemma haunting the experiences of contemporary African-American men:

> The stories must be told. Ideas of manhood, true and transforming, grow out of private, personal exchanges between fathers and sons. Yet for generations of black men in America this privacy, this privilege has been systematically breached in a most shameful and public way. Not only breached, but brutally usurped,

> mediated by murder, mayhem, misinformation. Generation after generation of black men, deprived of the voices of their fathers, are for all intents and purposes, born semi-orphans. Mama's baby, Daddy's maybe. Fathers in exile, in hiding, on the run, anonymous, undetermined, dead. The lost fathers cannot claim their sons, speak to them about growing up, until the fathers claim their own manhood. Speak first to themselves, then unambiguously to their sons. Arrayed against the possibility of conversation between fathers and sons is the country they inhabit, everywhere proclaiming the inadequacy of black fathers, their lack of manhood in almost every sense the term's understood here in America. (ibid.: 65)

What does it mean to be a father? What does it mean to be a black father? Who is this familiar stranger whose 'vastness I intuited but couldn't grasp' (ibid.: 77)? How do you start to tell his story when you know – or think you know – that fatherhood is 'the bitterness of [knowing] how close to winning losing can be' (ibid.: 43, 69)? Like the ties that bind Oedipus to Laius, what *Fatheralong* uncovers, or, more accurately, symptomatically reveals, is how racism is passed on from father to son, like an unwitting curse: a bitterness buried yet operative between them, inhabiting the son (though he doesn't know it), a faultline of self and identity. Hence the mark that the black father leaves, a mark that is both ineffaceable and irremediable. Typed, in the wider culture, as the cause of, and cure for, black men's 'failure', his father's apparently lost, and untellable, life is the story that the son must find and narrate if he is to begin to understand how, and why, blackness has come to represent an inheritable fault. Only by retelling father stories, Wideman suggests, can Afro-American men reestablish authentic worlds of communication, reopen lost channels of wisdom and counsel, intimacy and love. That's the redemptive privilege in finding, and listening to – but where? and how? – the paternal voices which have been mediated and murdered, usurped and witheld, by a culture, and a nation, intent on driving home to black men the inadequacy of black fathers: their weakness, their absence, their brutality, their death. Against that vision, or nightmare, *Fatheralong* is looking for new, and various, stories and storytellers, for a telling that cures by offering a form of collective black reminiscence: stories of origin and initiation which can run counter to the pornographic, often fatal, images of black men trafficked throughout white America.

In trying to tell the father's story, telling itself must become part of the plot, including African-American history as plot. In this sense, black men, black writers, are searching for a narrative, even fictional, cure for the traumas of history – in this case, father-history. In *Fatheralong*, Wideman sets out to retrieve (the always elusive) memories of his father, Edgar. 'He floats in and out of my recollections of growing up, like memory itself', he observes, reflecting on a childhood marked by Edgar's strange presence-absence (ibid.: 137). 'Hauntingly ambiguous', he continues, Edgar's 'presence and absence [were] two sides of a coin, and when you toss it to decide what really happened, it lands standing on edge' (ibid.). On edge, poised on the threshold of two irreconcilable outcomes, maddeningly unreachable even when close enough to touch, Wideman must gamble if he is to redeem his father's missing story: an impossible legacy, the story of his father's life represents a failure that cannot be gone beyond but which remains the only true path of manhood – literally, fatheralong – for Wideman, the son. But how do you tell the father's story when he is anonymous, absent, undetermined? Is his narrative, his legacy, to be decided by a mere toss of a coin? Wideman can only give voice to his father's story by acknowledging that voice as absent from its telling. As if Edgar's past and present failures of filial attachment, the bitter memories they produce, can only be reinvested by an act of narration which makes that father's untold tale unnarratable. This enigma is, no doubt, part of the black father's truth and story: father stories can only be avowed and told in so far as they go beyond narrative fulfillment, come down on the cusp between presence and absence. That is, if the black father is to be rescued – by himself, by his son – he must tell himself, poised as he is on the edge of recovery and oblivion. For the sake of his future, then, there are two traditions, two legacies that the black son must come to know and to recognise. One curtails, keeps desire at bay; the other nurtures – and connects, as Wideman puts it, 'what's momentary and passing to what surpasses, materiality to ideal' (ibid.: 63). Already breached by his father's haunting ambiguity, Wideman – cast in the role of archetypal black son – must seek out his father if he is to legitimate his future claims.

Two sides of a coin: the black father's public, and private, role as *gamble*, or ghost, as a matter of fraught speculation on the widening gulf between black men and cultural legitimacy (as a spectral presence on the threshold of seemingly endless generational conflict). Wideman's *Fatheralong* takes up its place in a black literature and cinema which puts the (sometimes) tortured relation between father and son at the centre of its imaginary and political project. What connects, say, Brent Staples' *Parallel Time* (1994) to Nathan McCall's

Makes Me Wanna Holler (1994), John Edgar Wideman's *Fatheralong* (1994) to John Singleton's film *Boyz N the Hood* (1991), is the scene of a more or less dazzling filial drama staged against the well-known charge that the 'Negro family' and, in particular, the black father, is cause for national concern. That charge found one of its most cogent, and offensive, statements in the Moynihan Report, *The Negro Family: the Case for National Action*, published in 1965. Following the leads already provided by Kenneth and Mamie Clark's *Dark Ghetto* and E. Franklyn Frazier's *The Negro Family in the United States* (1939), Daniel Patrick Moynihan insisted on the 'crushing burdens' on black men in families headed predominantly by women, of the 'tangle of pathology' inhabiting black family life. 'Negro children without fathers flounder – and fail', he proclaimed (Moynihan, cited in Rainwater and Yancey 1967: 35). They know no restraint, or discipline. Rootless, they are without origin. This issue of absent or inadequate paternity is never far from a cultural assessment – or narrative – of the nihilistic rage driving black men. In a society 'which presumes male leadership in private and public affairs', writes Moynihan, when families fail, societies fail; only fathers can quell the bafflement and violent turbulence of black children; only responsible fathers can be proper men (ibid.: 6).

Writing against a 'world without fathers', the 'Moynihan Report' became a key reference point for black artists and critics *writing back* to a country in which, as Wideman puts it in 1994, 'people of color walk under a cloud of unsettled paternity' (Wideman 1994: 82). 'Somewhere, lost in that cloud or separated from us by its darkness', Wideman concludes, 'our fathers reside' (ibid.: 83). 'Our fathers', black fathers – poignant symbols of loss and separation, of what is wrong with black cultures and black men. Or, to put it another way: a symptom, a damning performative where '"He's just like his Daddy" ... cuts through you like a razor' (George 1994a: 263). 'What is wrong with black fathers?' 'What is wrong with black men?': these questions loom over postwar American culture, part of a more pervasive anxiety about the decline of paternal authority, the so-called 'crisis' of masculinity in contemporary cultural life. A monumental crisis: for black men, the despair of living knowing that life itself is always in question, interfered with, disrupted by popular tirades filled, according to Nelson George, with 'negative expectations'(ibid.). It may be that black fathers, black sons, are carrying the burden of that anxiety – a burden which, going beyond the agon of the relation between father and son, has become central to black men's exploration of masculinity and manhood. How do you tell the father's story? Or, in Wideman's phrase, 'fatherstories'.

How do you overcome what Joseph Beam has described as a 'legacy of silence' between black fathers and sons? (Beam 1986: 235). By going back to the fatherstories told through the canonic texts of African-American literature, perhaps, testing those stories against the silence being played out between black men, fathers and sons, brothers and brothers, in the literature and cinema of the 1990s. Let's take our cue from Wideman who, 'learn[ing] to resist those who would come between us', turns to two of the most influential thinkers of the 'inadequacy, the failures of his black fathers': Richard Wright and James Baldwin (Wideman 1994: 72). Two writers who, struggling to write themselves out from the shadows of their fathers, depict a world increasingly hostile to black male claims for equality and legitimacy. Disobedient, rebellious sons whose filial dramas are central to African-American literary history and whose autobiographies of youth and childhood offer us a point of view from which contemporary desires to reclaim the black father can be seen as enacting an uncanny repetition (or at least, psychoanalytically speaking, a deferred affect).

I

'If *Black Boy* doesn't exactly slay the father, it radically displaces him': Wideman's commentary on Richard Wright's famous autobiography concludes by restating a critical consensus: namely, that Wright repudiates the brute legacy of his sharecropper father, Richard Nathan Wright, and, in so doing, orphans himself (ibid.: 73). That is, Wright's displacement of the father for his 'inadequacy' and 'failures' is not, or not only, a parricide; it is also a claim for illegitimacy (ibid.: 72). Even if the function of *Black Boy* is, as Wright's biographer, Michael Fabre, attests 'to slay the father symbolically', or, as Robert Stepto puts it in *From Behind the Veil*, 'to not so much slay his father as bury him alive', Wright's attempts to inter, to murder, his father – to proclaim himself an orphan, to bury his father alive – is inseparably linked to the ruse of self-narrating (narration staked, in turn, on Wright's bid for freedom) (Fabre 1985: 78; Stepto 1979: 138). In short, in *Black Boy*, Wright's parricidal wishes support his attempt to tell, and write, himself into a different family romance. Why, for example, symbolically preserve the father in memory if the desire is to bury or forget him, to relinquish, via recollection, everything that he represents? Or, to put the question another way: what exactly does Wright give up in order to free himself from his father's past? Certainly, Wright's representation of his father in *Black Boy* seems to be inextricable from, and impossible without, a certain kind of forgetting of his father's 'crude and raw past' (Wright 1945: 43). A forgetting which records and openly condemns (and which insists on remembering) the failures and inadequacies of black (and white) paternal authority as such.

First published in 1945, and originally subtitled 'A Record of Southern Childhood', *Black Boy* is a type of political self-analysis, an attempt to write through the experience of a deeply repressed childhood lived out in the context of the race hysteria of the Southern States of America during the 1920s. 'I wrote the book to tell a series of incidents strung through my childhood', Wright notes in *PM* magazine in 1945, 'but the main desire was to render a judgement on my environment': that is, the spiritual and cultural impoverishment of the South, of black men in the South, the hunger and distress caused by a deserting father (Wright, cited in Fabre 1973: 252). In *Black Boy,* that judgement entails an unambiguous rejection of the South along with Wright's father, absent since Wright's early childhood. 'When I tried to talk to him', Wright recalls, 'I realized that, though ties of blood made us kin, though I could see a shadow of my face in his face, though there was an echo of my voice in his voice, we were forever strangers, speaking a different language, living on vastly different planes of reality' (Wright 1945: 42). Strange, stranger, 'the image of my father', he writes, 'possessed some vital meaning which always eluded me' (ibid.: 30). That elusiveness, neither present nor absent, is associated with feelings of conflict and fear. 'I am dimly aware', he recalls in an earlier version of *Black Boy*, 'that I felt a vague dread of him' (Wright, cited in Fabre 1973: 11). Vague, diffuse, without clarity, the image of his father, though 'real and tangible enough', 'always seemed, in my mind, to exist far away' (ibid.). Acting as an elusive metonym for his inarticulate and brutalised childhood self – a self before literacy and freedom – it will take Wright twenty-five years to escape that image: it will take Chicago and the North, Marxism and psychoanalysis, literature and writing, for Wright to learn how to come to terms with, and renounce, finally, his 'black peasant' father; twenty-five years to bury alive the meaning of his father which possesses him (Wright 1945: 43). Identifying that meaning with the racial violence and cultural sickness of the South to which it responds – identifying his father with the sickness of race segregation – Wright narrates the plot of his life as one caught between resistance and repression.

Like *Fatheralong*, *Black Boy* explores the impact of racism on black father–son relations but, in Wright's book, the telling which cures is the one that exorcises the father – that murders him at the crossroads between slavery, legacy and the freedom of a literary life. At the close of the first chapter, for example, Wright describes a return journey he made to see his father in Natchez, Mississippi, after an absence of twenty-five years. It's a scene of return that will be repeated, reenacted, and worked through his various writings on black men as subsumed and haunted by racism's inescapable legacies: once again, black men at war with themselves, caught, as he puts it in 'How Bigger was Born', in a 'No Man's Land' (Wright 1983 :27).[1] 'A quarter of a century was to elapse between the time when I saw my father ... and the time when I was to see him again', he writes, 'a quarter of a century during which my mind and my consciousness had become so greatly and violently altered ...':

> That day a quarter of a century later when I visited him on the plantation – he was standing against the sky, smiling toothlessly, his hair whitened, his body bent, his eyes glazed with dim recollection, his fearsome aspect of twenty-five years ago gone forever from him – I was overwhelmed to realize that he could never understand me or the scalding experiences that had swept me beyond his life and into an area of living that he could never know. I stood before him, poised, my mind aching as it embraced the simple nakedness of his life, feeling how completely his soul was imprisoned by the slow flow of the seasons, by wind and rain and sun, how fastened were his memories to a crude and raw past, how chained were his actions and emotions to the direct, animalistic impulses of his withering body ...
>
> From far beyond the horizons that bound this bleak plantation there had come to me through my living the knowledge that my father was a black peasant who had gone to the city seeking life, but who had failed in the city; a black peasant who had been hopelessly snarled in the city; a black peasant who had at last fled the city – that same city that had lifted me in its burning arms and borne me toward alien and undreamed-of shores of knowing. (ibid.: 42, 43)

A quarter of a century, and it doesn't get any easier, whether in memory or narrative, to dispose of the black father's (dis)inheritance. As a country boy done good in the city, Wright can only show how far he's come, can only make his success narratable, by projecting himself beyond his father's horizons. But that projective self, unashamedly and, at first glance, utterly without irony, can only show itself through a prolepsis: 'A quarter of a century was to lapse ...'. Looking back on itself, the autobiographical, or narrating,

I is forced to measure and to use time differently. Interrupting itself, Wright's narrative time is time future, a proleptic time matured and scalded by harsh life experience, going beyond his father's mythic slave time of the preindustrial. In 'How Jim Crow Feels', first published in 1947, Wright spoke of this encounter with his father on a Mississippi plantation in terms of a gap between unavowable kinship and wished-for community:

> I discovered that blood and race alone were not sufficient to knit people together in a community of feeling. The psychological gap between us which had been wrought by time made us regard one another with tension and forced smiles and I knew that it was not the myth of blood but of continuous associations, shared ideals and kindred intentions that made people one. (Wright 1947a: 27)

And yet, if inheritance is all about continuities rather than gaps, idealities and intentions rather than myths, this is no simple parricide or symbolic burial. If when we first meet him, the father is treated as a metonym for *all* the oppressive failures of the South – against which Wright defines the undreamed-of, redeeming time of the Northern city – in the concluding pages of *Black Boy*, Wright will also comment: 'I was not leaving the South to forget the South but so that some day I might understand it, might come to know what its rigors had done to me, to its children' (Wright 1945: 284). Remembering in order to forget, or to inter, Wright wrote *Black Boy* as a way of disposing of those 'rigors', to exorcise the South's 'sprawling land of unconscious suffering' (Wright 1977: 7). Upon reflection, his endless preoccupation with what in 'How Bigger Was Born' he refers to as the 'weird and paradoxical birth' of the Negro in America, is associated not only with the psychic and social death he experiences growing up in the South – a culture which had reduced his father to a 'creature of the earth', with 'no regrets and no hope' – but also with the Negro's ambivalent relation to modernity (ibid.: 30). In this sense, the autobiographical *I* of *Black Boy* appears as a representative attempt to articulate the dumb yearnings of the South's black boys, to retrieve his own father's inarticulate failures. 'I wanted to give voice, lend my tongue to the voiceless Negro boys', he says, straightforwardly, in that *PM* interview in 1945. 'I feel that way about the deprived children of the South' (Wright 1945a: 3). Giving voice to black children (or, more precisely, to black boys), lending them his tongue, it is as if Wright is adopting the orphans brought into being by the brutal racism of the South – an act of paternity and narration (narration as paternity), which, in

1946, in his Introduction to Horace Cayton's and St. Clair Drake's *Black Metropolis*, Wright will bring into contact with the figure of Hamlet by recalling his dying words to Horatio. 'And in this harsh world draw thy breath in pain/ To tell my story': Hamlet's well-known lines become a literary, and legitimising, precedent for Wright's own 'dumb yearning to write, to tell my story, even though I did not know what my story was' (Wright 1946: xvii).

Equating his arrival in the North with his birth as a writer, then, Wright twins his wish to give voice to those dumb yearnings with his rejection of his father's cultural disinheritance. That rejection, voiced in parenthesis in *Black Boy*, extends his father's disinheritance to African-American culture as a whole: '(Negroes had never been allowed to catch the full spirit of Western Civilization ... they lived somehow in it but not of it)' (Wright 1945: 45). In a contemporary review of *Black Boy*, W. E. B. Du Bois found that judgement too 'harsh and forbidding'; but you might say (with Wideman) that in this desperate, ultimately doomed attempt to run away from the image of a brutal, illiterate father – a father whose legacy 'pursued him, caught up with him, taunted him' – Wright found it necessary to orphan himself out of the regressive violence of his Southern family romance (Du Bois 1945: 132; Wideman 1994: 72, 73). Kill or be killed: 'if I did not leave, I would perish', Wright states, baldly, in 1945, 'either because of possible violence of others against me, or because of my possible violence against them' (Wright 1945: 282). On the other hand, Wright's journey to articulacy and freedom appears to be already foreclosed by a return to his father's past, a return which also belongs to his future. Quite literally: Wright's return to his father in Natchez, Mississippi, is a way of making reparation for his yet unmastered future; a recovery, so to speak, of the writing yet to come. In other words, for Wright, a repudiation of the father and his culture is not only about breaking a circle of violence derived from that father's unwitting complicity with white racism; it is also about renouncing a certain kind of violently repressive black masculinity, one devoid of 'loyalty, of sentiment, of tradition', and chained to the bestial simplicity of 'direct, animalistic impulses': a masculinity outside the plot of history, literally dumb (ibid.: 43). Deeply suspicious of his father's inheritance – in which all white men were 'Misters', and all black men 'boys' – Wright gives voice to his ambivalence towards a father, and towards father-figures, who, trapped in a time-warp, want to be called 'Mister'. These are fathers who identify with the racist violence of (white) culture in the South by miming that violence in their relations with their black sons. Fathers who want to imprison (inter?) their sons in the 'flat, repetitive present' of lives lived without regret or hope (Fabre 1985: 80). Wright has nothing but contempt for, and fear at, his father's desire to be 'the lawgiver in the family', a desire which is seen as a continuation of the murderously 'loud' violence he encounters, over and over again, as a child and youth (Wright 1945: 16). Rejecting the present tense of his father's story, Wright plots his story as a return whose destiny is always to go forward. The direction of his flight – from the South, from his father – is consistently thematised as a journey turned rearward, a journey which reverses the spectacle of his father's failure in order to evoke and recapture his paternal dream of undreamed-of shores of knowing. A displaced figure throughout his fictional memoir, Wright thus ends by deliberately making himself an outcast, cutting himself off from the 'essential bleakness' of black life in the South, divorcing himself from his father's violent patrimony (ibid.: 45).

And, I think, from the shock, or trauma, of that life. What Wright will not let out of his sight, or field of vision, are the 'violent shocks of Southern living' and Southern manhood – shocks which, running through his writing, are passed on to those black writers who come in his wake: among others, James Baldwin, Ralph Ellison, John Edgar Wideman. To take up Wright's literary legacy, then, is also to take on his restless questioning of black paternity, to journey back to the father's roots in the hope of finding a more redeeming future. It is to become involved in stories of black fathers and sons, stories impelled by the necessity to dispute the degraded rights of paternity.

In 1963, Irving Howe published 'Black Boys and Native Sons', an essay which charges both James Baldwin and Ralph Ellison with a 'filial betrayal' of Wright. In 'The World and the Jug', an immediate, and furious, response to Howe's essay, Ellison set out his reasons for his unequivocal rejection of Wright's literary legacy (Ellison 1967: 141, 113). Opting for Hemingway as his artistic 'ancestor', as the model of the 'true father-as-artist' he aspires to be, Ellison consigns Wright to the role of a mere 'relative', a lesser affiliation which he invites us to read as a mere contingency of birth and of blackness (ibid.: 140). For Ellison, it seems, paternity is a matter of metaphor rather than kinship; or, more precisely, the act of literature is one that allows the son to write his way into new kin, to found his father, or family, of choice. At the same time, Ellison is uncertain; he vacillates between Hemingway and Wright (does he suspect that Hemingway might not see him as the ideal son?) in a way that troubles this vision of literature, and literary influence, as the son's wilful interracial family romance: as Ellison puts it, it seems to be a case of 'heads you win, tails you lose' (ibid.: 140, 142). You could derive a law of African-American literary succession from that double bind, the (fixed) gamble which recalls Wideman's metaphor of paternity as coin, as a strictly unwinnable outcome. In relation to an 'untrue' father, the son is faced with a choice: loyalty or betrayal, identification or resistance. It is tempting to see the price of that gamble in terms of an inescapable, and costly, legacy: the pressure of being a 'Negro' *and* a 'writer', as Ellison puts it, 'has cost me quite a pretty penny' (ibid.: 142).

In 1963, Baldwin does not respond to Howe's charge. But taking a long look back on his origins as a writer in 'The Price of the Ticket', first published in 1985, Baldwin returns once again to what he describes as the legacy of the 'conundrum of color': 'to use that inheritance, precisely, to claim the birthright from which that inheritance had so brutally and specifically excluded me' (Baldwin 1998: 810). '*Know whence you came*', Baldwin enjoins himself, repeating a refrain which runs throughout his work and takes the story back to Baldwin's relations with Wright – his one time spiritual father and mentor – in Paris in the late 1940s and early 1950s (ibid.: 841). Wideman picks up on the fact that in *Notes of a Native Son*, a collection of essays first published in 1955, Baldwin 'felt the necessity to remove himself from Richard Wright's spiritual, literary paternity'; at the same time, I want to suggest, this is a title which locates Baldwin firmly as Wright's literary son (Wideman 1994: 73). Indeed, the filial drama played out between Wright's novel *Native Son* and Baldwin's *Notes of a Native Son*, is at once simple and remarkably complex – and one which, I want to suggest, allows us a glimpse into the dazzling filial drama Baldwin enacted with Wright.

'Notes of a Native Son', the essay which lends the collection its title, is a memoir to Baldwin's own embittered father – a confounding of the position of actual and literary fathers, and sons, which can be found throughout Baldwin's writings on Wright: the filiation, and disaffiliation, the play with an Oedipal narrative, that, he acknowledges, Wright could see far more clearly than he dared to (Baldwin 1964: 156). Reflecting on his father in 1976, in an interview with the inmates of Riker's Island Prison, Baldwin spoke of how he was impelled by a need to 'understand the forces, the experience, the life that shaped him ... before I could grow up myself, before I could become a writer' (Baldwin 1976a: 55). As he puts it in 'Notes of a Native Son', the legacy of his father's 'intolerable bitterness of spirit' was that 'nothing is ever escaped', that what was his 'now was mine', to be endured (or, like Oedipus, fulfilled)

(Baldwin 1964: 73, 94). The scene is chastening enough, announcing a type of repetition and destiny, a traumatic bond which will also come to define Baldwin's relationship to Wright (ibid.: 94). Not only will Wright endure in Baldwin's fiction and essays, he will also continue to resist Baldwin's efforts to give him a proper burial, to utter his last rites. Take, for example, Baldwin's memorial essay, 'Alas, Poor Richard', first published in 1961 and collected in *Nobody Knows My Name: More Notes of a Native Son* (still harping on fathers?) (1991). Troping himself as that other well-known Oedipal son, Hamlet, Baldwin casts Wright in the role of Yorick: a dead jester on whose shoulder he once rode, now reduced to a skull – eyeless, tongueless, unable to give voice to the stories that, in his own identification with Hamlet, Wright had so clearly wanted to tell. (Is this a struggle about who gets to play the Dane?)

Like Hamlet, Baldwin's gorge rises at the memory of the intimacy between himself and Wright, an intimacy which gave way to abhorrence and mutual distrust when, in June 1949, Baldwin decided to publish the essay 'Everybody's Protest Novel' in which he attacks Wright's *Native Son* for its 'theology' of blackness. In 'Alas, Poor Richard', Baldwin returns to the scene of that rupture – a rupture doubly painful for Wright who, ironically enough, had not only advised and supported Baldwin in his struggles to give voice to himself as a writer, but had also helped him to place the essay with the Parisian journal, *Zero*. As Baldwin recalls it:

> Richard accused me of having betrayed him, and not only him but all American Negroes by attacking the idea of protest literature. It simply had not occurred to me that the essay could be interpreted in that way. I was still in the stage when I imagined that whatever was clear to me had only to be pointed out to become immediately clear to everyone. I was young enough to be proud of the essay and, sad and incomprehensible as it now sounds, I really think that I had rather expected to be patted on the head for my original point of view. It had not occurred to me that this point of view, which I had come to, after all, with some effort and some pain, could be looked on as treacherous and subversive. Again, I had mentioned Richard's *Native Son* at the end of the essay because it was the most important and most celebrated novel of Negro life to have appeared in America. Richard thought that I had attacked it, whereas as far as I was concerned, I had scarcely even criticised it. And Richard thought that I was trying to destroy his novel and his reputation; but it had not entered my mind that either of these *could* be destroyed,

> and certainly not by me. And yet, what made the interview so ghastly was not merely the foregoing or the fact that I could find no words with which to defend myself. What made it most painful was that Richard was right to be hurt, I was wrong to have hurt him. He saw clearly enough, far more clearly than I had dared to allow myself to see, what I had done: I had used his work as a kind of springboard into my own. His work was a road-block in my road, the sphinx, really, whose riddles I had to answer before I could become myself. (Baldwin 1991: 160–1)

In this passage, Baldwin is Oedipus, striving to reverse the disturbing journey of an initiation at the hands of Wright's riddling sphinx. But – and his writing alerts us to this – Baldwin is no straight Oedipus, killing the father for access to the mother. When Baldwin identifies Wright with the Sphinx, the riddle on the obstacle to his progress as a writer – a block to himself and his origins as a writer – he identifies the older man-father with a monstrous female, and not a father (after all, Oedipus unwittingly kills his father *before* meeting the Sphinx). Moreover, Oedipus encounters his father at a crossroads and not a roadblock. No matter: the disastrous effects of the deciphered riddle are the same *for all concerned*. Perhaps the important point here is that, though always acting on his reason, Baldwin, like Oedipus, is always *unwitting* in relation to Wright, his father; he kills him unknowingly in fulfilment of a curse laid against them both: Laius-Wright, Baldwin-Oedipus. Follow Oedipus's story backwards, as it were, and you discover the origin of that curse in the father's homosexual fault. As a young man, Laius develops a passion for Chrysippus, the son of King Pelops, and runs off with him. He – Laius – is cursed by Pelops, while Chrysippus dies of shame.[2] A fateful history, this, in which the father's sexual transgression turns his son into an instrument of mythic vengeance – a history that (perhaps unwittingly) Baldwin writes into his relationship with Wright. Even though he does not have the words with which to defend himself against Wright's charge, Baldwin is driven to displace him as Hamlet-Oedipus – as the monstrous and feminine sphinx in whose riddle lies a clue to his future.

If 'Everybody's Protest Novel' unknowingly solves the riddle of *Native Son*, it's a solution which must remove Wright as the obstacle on Baldwin's road to becoming a writer. Nevertheless, and perhaps naively, Baldwin still hoped to secure Wright's paternal love by his dazzling exploit: 'I think, in fact, that I counted on this coming about in some mysterious, irrevocable way, the way a child dreams of winning, by means of some dazzling exploit, the love of his parents' (ibid.: 156). 'Everybody's Protest Novel' is the dazzling exploit that fails to win the father's love, but succeeds in unravelling the riddle of Wright's *Native Son* and thereby discharging his literary debt to the older and more famous writer: the irony of slaying Wright by 'out-Wrighting' (in Ralph Ellison's memorable pun) Richard. It is as if that irony frees Baldwin as a writer, unleashing pain and anger, rather than respect and love, in Wright. In one sense, Baldwin's initiatory journey is like the end of *Hamlet*, littered with the corpses of formerly loved friends and rivals. Resolution here appears to present itself not only as a patricidal repetition of history but as a regretful scene of initiation: 'The saddest thing about our relationship is that my only means of discharging my debt to Richard was to become a writer' (ibid.: 156). Heads I win, tails you lose: parodying Wright-Laius as Sphinx-Yorick, Baldwin can thus live out and disavow the murderous edge to his emulation on his triumphant journey as a writer. Alas, poor Richard: alas, indeed!

If anything, Baldwin's rejection of Wright's protest fiction, its political (not to say, cathartic) agenda for the divided, warring conscious-unconscious personality of blacks, begins and ends with the image of persecutory fathers. Discussing Baldwin's semi-autobiographical novel, *Go Tell It On The Mountain*, first published in 1953, Michel Fabre, in 'Fathers and Sons', notes that Baldwin's fictions evolve around a 'constellation of fathers': 'unknown and mythical father, real and legitimate father, putative father, possible father, adulterous husband and father of a bastard' (Fabre 1974: 124). Begun in 1943 and continuously redrafted over the next ten years – the same period during which he met, and was encouraged in his writing by, Wright in Harlem, New York – it may be no coincidence that Baldwin's working title for this novel was *In My Father's House*. To push the point, as a disobedient, murderous son, Baldwin's relation to Wright's work exemplifies the massive double bind of identity and identification (which is not to say that he was always fully aware of the unresolved filial drama between them, or of its impact on the generalised scene of his writing). In 'Many Thousands Gone', for example, first published in 1951, and collected in *Notes of a Native Son*, Baldwin's critique of Wright's *Native Son* pictures its protagonist, Bigger Thomas, as Wright's Oedipal son: the 'monstrosity' of his image, the blackness that condemns him, becomes the 'herald of disaster', makes 'his end inevitable' (Baldwin 1964: 32, 30). If 'in our image of the Negro breathes the past we deny', he continues, Bigger's 'fantastic and fearful image' performs an unwitting reflection of the 'fantasy Americans hold in their minds when they speak of a Negro' – a fantasy which prevents them from seeing that 'all men are betrayed by greed and guilt and blood-lust', that 'no-one's hands are clean' (ibid.: 22, 26, 34). The deferred effects of that fantasy, one that treats Bigger as a representative *type*, is not simply a question of denial, or forgetting: after all, 'Oedipus did not remember the throngs that bound his feet; nevertheless the marks they left testified to that doom toward which his feet were leading him' (ibid.: 22). If blackness is the familial mark which binds him, if 'black is the color of damnation', Baldwin concludes, 'this is his only possible end' (ibid.: 33). For Baldwin, therefore, *Native Son* collapses life into tragic legend, recognition into disavowal, and Bigger Thomas becomes a cipher for white America's Oedipal 'estrangement' from the racially interlinked bloodlines of its past (ibid.: 19).

All Americans, then, and not just people of colour, walk under a cloud of unsettled paternity: America's family romance is an illegitimate '*blood* relationship' (ibid.: 32). Perhaps this is why Wideman, in *Fatheralong*, writes: 'Black fathers, white fathers, both, neither. Submission, rejection, adoption, upstaging, replacing. Black American men seeking surrogate fathers in other countries, continents', in 'gang families ... where the idea of fathers and sons is anachronistic, redundant', replaced by sons bonded to other sons in fraternal brotherhoods (Wideman 1994: 75). In the remainder of this chapter, I want to start to clarify that shift from father-son to brother by turning to John Singleton's *Boyz N the Hood* (1991): a film driven by the brother-son's search for a language of selfhood and survival outside of the ghetto culture of the 'hood', a search driven by love of a father. Credited with the creation of an 'Afrocentric father fantasy cinema', *Boyz* is *Black Boy* told in reverse – ending with a romantic, neo-nationalist return to the father after the death of the brother-son (George 1994: 117). To put this another way: fraternal ties in *Boyz* are thoroughly implicated in, if not indissociable from, black father stories. Taking the form of a demand on the son not to join a gang family, *Boyz*'s father stories are also intimately bound up with narratives proclaiming the black father's redemptive love.

2

At the very end of *Boyz*, Doughboy, played by the rapper, Ice Cube, says to his lifelong friend, Tre Styles (Cuba Golding Jr): 'I ain't got no brother. Got no mother, neither'. To which Tre responds: 'You still got one brother left, man'. Moments later and before the final screen credits, a caption appears announcing Doughboy's death, two weeks later, the victim of a drive-by gangland shooting. Bringing the narrative, and that intimate, even halting, exchange between 'brothers', to a close, that announcement echoes the caption which opens the film to the sound of yet another gangland shooting: 'One out of every twenty-one Black American males will be murdered in their lifetime'. Next frame: 'Most will die at the hands of another Black male'. We hear a young boy whimpering: 'They shot my brother, they shot my brother'.

In one sense, Doughboy's statement and his death provide a *finis* to the film's main dynamic: the deaths of 'brothers', actual or adopted, the 'genocidal' crisis of young African-American men which frames and drives *Boyz N the Hood* – a source of identification, and pain, for its black spectators. 'Most black Americans could see themselves somewhere in this film', writes Nelson George in *Blackface: Reflections on African-Americans and the Movies* in 1994. '*Boyz*, more than any of the other 1991 films, was able to satisfy both young audiences and their parents'; Michele Wallace describes her experience of seeing *Boyz* as devastating: she left the cinema in tears, 'crying for all the dead men in my family' (Nelson George 1994a: 119; Wallace 1992: 123). Others left the cinema equally devastated, but in more violent mood. The opening weekend of *Boyz* saw thirty people wounded; 600 filmgoers in Racine, Wisconsin, started a mini-riot and looting spree after seeing the movie; the fatal shooting of a man in Riverdale, Chicago occurred while the movie was running, and another man was shot dead at a screening in Minneapolis. If watching the drama and tragedy of *Boyz* unfold was, Wallace observes, 'like watching the last act of *Hamlet*', the film also seemed to compel its early audience to confuse stage and screen, to mistake the real for the imagined (ibid.: 123). Unable to resist the spectacle of black-on-black murder, it is as if this early response to *Boyz* was the same response as seeing the murder of one's flesh and blood, the fraternal violence on screen now part of the audience, to be carried within them as they left the darkened theatre.

A black, male and urban coming-of-age film – the story focuses on three black teenagers in South Central LA – *Boyz* appears to have become a privileged instance of cinematic recognition, and mourning, for its African-American audiences. Like a mirror, in fact, if we follow Lisa Kennedy's reading of the film in 'The Body in Question': like Spike Lee's cinema, Kennedy suggests, *Boyz* has been treated 'as something of a hand-held mirror by the collective body – many of us drawn to his [Singleton's] images less like Narcissus than like people who have seldom seen themselves' (Kennedy 1992: 109). Acknowledging, and displacing, one of the dominant accounts of the relation between spectator and screen in the psychoanalytic film theory of the 1970s – crudely, cinema as a site for narcissistic recognition of an ideal image of self on screen – Kennedy casts the black spectator as one deprived of, and so to drawn to, that self as it starts to emerge through the black cinema of the 1980s and 1990s.[3] Like a 'hand-held' mirror – rather than, say, the static, and immobilising, screen invested by some psychoanalytic film theory – that cinema *moves* around: it can be used to make its black spectators visible, from different angles, different views, like the last act of *Hamlet*. '[C]inema has now become a house of mirrors', Kennedy concludes, multiplying the perspectives, 'with every viewing, the black community gets an inkling of its shape, its texture, even its age and gender (mostly young, mostly male these days)' (ibid.).

Mostly young, mostly male: is this Hollywood as a cinema of male adolescence (what the New German Cinema film-maker, Alexander Kluge, would call 'kids' pictures'? (Kluge, cited in Lebeau 1995: 30)). 'Youth is a prevailing theme of this era of black film', writes Nelson George, 'the young filmmakers are obsessed with writing about themselves and how they see the world' (George 1994: 117) Perhaps, but *Boyz* must also complicate the model of fulfilled masculine narcissism which has so often been used to support a critical repudiation of contemporary youth cinema. After all, these young black men are dead, or, more precisely, they are waiting to die – a fatality which may start to skew those accounts of the fascinated, and cathartic, *pleasures* of recognising oneself on the screen. There may be recognition here, but it's deeply painful, drawn back into the vicissitudes of a deadly, and fraternal, family romance: 'You still got one brother left, man' (but not for long). As both narrative and cinematic event, the fate of black men – of dead black men – preoccupies this film, troubling, I think, those attempts to read the film through the frame of Oedipal anxiety. In his brief, but important, reading of *Boyz* in 'It's a Family Affair', for example, Paul Gilroy identifies the film's appeal in its representation of an Oedipal anxiety that, he suggests, is now dominating black political and cultural life: in other words, that 'crisis' in black masculinity which gives rise to the desire to return to the father as privileged symbol of community, race and nation ('Larry Fishburne-style patriarchal power that held these different local forms of blackness together' (Gilroy 1993: 198)). In Gilroy's view, that symbol, or fiction, of the father can be sustained only by treating the politics of race as the politics of family (the Moynihan move) and, further, by asking young black men to stand in for the African-American experience as such. 'Family has come to stand for community, for race, for nation', he continues. 'It is a kind of short-cut to solidarity. The discourse of family and the discourse of nation are very closely connected' (ibid.: 203). Hence the fantasmatic, and conservative, reconstruction of both through the 'ideal heterosexual family' that Gilroy finds on display throughout *Boyz N the Hood* (ibid.: 205).

Gilroy's fascination is with the film's main focus on Tre's self-fashioning through his father, Furious (played by Larry Fishburne), and Furious' self-fashioning through learning to be a father to his son: as Michael Eric Dyson puts it in *Making Malcolm*, *Boyz* is all about fathers and sons who re-create each other from mutual need and desire. The film's message, Dyson concludes, is that 'black men must raise black boys if they are to become healthy black men' (Dyson 1995: 112). At one point, Furious says to Tre: 'Any fool with a dick can make a baby, but only a real man can raise his children'. The prospect of raising a son is also presented as what saves Furious from the criminal and violent fates of his childhood friends in the 'hood: 'I wanted to be somebody you could look up to'. Or, the son is the father of the father. On one level, Gilroy's criticism is unanswerable: an idealisation of the father and of masculinity has been making itself felt through black writing and cinema for decades.[4] African-American cinema is, in this view, virtually a father itself, offering its paternal fantasy as both lure and spectacle, filmic and social solution. At the same time, Gilroy's powerful focus on the Oedipal-patriarchal as a figure which occludes the difference, and diversity, of African-American lives, passes over too quickly the preoccupation with death, with the father as a defence against death, which runs through *Boyz* and its anxious idealisation of the brother-father. Oedipus collapses father into brother so far as his children are concerned – 'Come feel your brother's hands. It was their work/ That darkened these clear eyes – your father's eyes' (Sophocles, *Oedipus Rex* 1515–16).) In other words, if *Boyz* is a type of collective therapy – an attempt, as Gilroy puts it, 'to compensate and rebuild the race by instituting appropriate forms of masculinity and male authority' – then, in its own terms, the film has to act as a defence against the very genocidal crisis it identifies (Gilroy 1993: 203). But does it? Can it? Can fathers, or films, really defend their sons against one another? Or, more precisely, can a father defend his son against the fate of becoming a dead brother? – the fate which, at the heart of *Boyz N the Hood*, is re-registered in the shootings which greeted the opening of the film?

This is, I think, the question that the film asks itself (though I'm not sure that it provides an answer). 'I ain't got no brother. Got no mother, neither': the two absences which Doughboy identifies at the very end of the film should really be three. After all, he's missing a father too. In contrast to Tre, whose coming-of-age is presented throughout the film in relation to the nurturing presence of Furious, Doughboy witnesses the gangland murder of his only brother, Ricky (Morris Chestnutt), and experiences rejection from his mother (Tyra Ferrell) who tells him: 'You ain't shit. Just like your Daddy'. But what I most wish to stress in this reading of *Boyz* as a type of fraternal romance is how Tre's wish to rename himself as a brother at the film's close cryptically unfolds that dynamic. If we take the climactic scene of the film – Doughboy's revenge gangland killing of Ricky's murderers – Tre's refusal to take part in this 'fraternal' execution is clearly presented as the result of his father's example. (*Boyz* underlines the point visually by intercutting shots of an anxious Furious with images of the gang cruising in the car looking for Ricky's killers.) In short, Tre's refusal is what saves him from the same fraternal bonds in whose name he adopts the doomed, semi-orphaned Doughboy at the film's close. In *Boyz*, we are thus made to witness the difference between being a brother with a father and the numerous fatherless brothers who populate the film. That difference is presented as the result of Tre's redemption as Furious' son and, by contrast, Doughboy's fatal adoption of the fraternities of the 'hood after his degrading rejection by his mother: 'You ain't shit. Just like your Daddy'.

The film's narrative is thus acting out the Oedipal implications of Doughboy's semi-orphan status in terms of a tension (again, we are in the world of Moynihan) between real and adopted brothers, present and absent fathers, bad and good-enough mothers. And yet, at several key moments in the film, *Boyz* also offers a critique of its investment in 'Afrocentric father fantasy cinema' (George 1994a: 117). In the course of an exchange between Furious and Tre's mother, Reva (played by Angela Bassett), she says:

> You taught him to be a man. I'll give you that, because most men aren't man enough to do what you did. ... What you did is no different from what mothers have been doing since the beginning of time. It's just too bad more brothers won't do the same. But don't think you're special.

The shifts here from father to brother to mother end up presenting fatherhood as the ultimate form of fraternal mothering. If, as the film suggests, only the father can bear the son alive, in this exchange it is only in so far as he is a brother who does what a mother does: mothers have always been 'man enough' to raise their children since the beginning of time. If *Boyz* represents an idealised paternal fantasy, in other words, that investment is also shown to be profoundly unstable, unable to sustain the father's demarcation from the fatedness of brothers, and fraternal ties from a mother's love.

In one of the opening scenes of the film, for example, Tre is shocked awake by the sound of Furious firing several shots at the figure of a retreating burglar, who escapes. Escorting Tre outside to await the arrival of the police, Furious says: 'I aimed right for his head', to which Tre responds: 'You should've blown it off'. Furious' response is significant: 'Don't say that. It'd just be killing another brother'. In other words, the father's right to kill a brother in defense of a son cannot be passed on to the son. At the same time, Furious' sense of what it means to kill legitimately in the name of true brotherhood confirms the film's presentation of Doughboy, whose abandonment by a father condemns him to a cycle of fratricidal violence. To put this another way: Furious' right to murder a brother, out of filial love, emerges as the film's inability to sustain an absolute, non-negotiable limit between brother-sons and present-absent fathers. These tensions thus complicate Gilroy's and Kennedy's belief that *Boyz* acts primarily as a narcissistic mirror for black men searching for lost fathers, a belief that simplifies the film's loving epitaph to brother-sons killed in the 'hood and its image of the brother-father as good-enough mother. Further, given the haunting ambiguity of fathers in stories about black manhood, the mournful-murderous response to *Boyz* by African–American spectators suggests something altogether different from self-obsessed narcissistic recognition. In its depiction of an anomic, lost generation of brothers and sons, *Boyz* represents a more nuanced response to the complex legacies of the black father in America.

It goes without saying, perhaps, that father stories are part of the wider histories and rhetorics used by Afro-America in its search for clues to its future, and the deeper meanings of its past. In 'Father Stories', the conclusion to *Fatheralong*, Wideman describes these stories as ones 'that take us back, that bring us here, where you are, where I am, needing to make sense, to go on if we can and should' (Wideman 1994: 178). Making sense, going on: race and memory as part of the continuous narrative joining black fathers and sons, including Wideman's own son, Jake, now serving a life-sentence for the murder of another black man. In *Boyz*, Furious, cast in the role of black nationalist, presents that narrative in a speech on life in the 'hood, the gunshops and liquor stores which sell death to young black men. 'They want us to kill ourselves', he announces to the small crowd of brothers and sisters who gather around him. 'You're doing exactly what they want you to do. You got to think about your future, young brother'. This is angry, or furious, speech: a speech which reads the life of black men in terms of the others – 'they' – who wish to see them dead: black men as men who, not thinking about their future, conform to somebody else's desire that they kill themselves. As such, and crucially, *Boyz* shows up how father-brother-son stories are already possessed by the murderous fantasies of the social tie. That is, *Boyz* bears witness to how the 'hood, or more strongly, Afro-America, has literally become the last act of *Hamlet*. If, as Wideman argues in *Fatheralong*, father stories must be told to break down the walls between 'the two of us, father and son, son and father', that is because we need the father as a defence against that death wish, that spectacle of black men, dead or mutilated, before a crowd of spectators. 'The stories [of the black father's disinheritance] must be told', Wideman suggests, because 'the part of him I dreaded [was] also the deepest bond' (ibid.: 134). 'Tattletale proof in the pudding', father stories represent a 'broken circle – unbroken' not only between father and son, but between fantasy and culture (ibid.: 50, 71). In this case, if the politics of the race is also a politics of the family in contemporary Afro-American culture, the father is there to mediate between those forced to act out the Oedipal plot, or family romance, of black *Hamlet*, and those who get to remain in their seats: offstage, looking on. No surprise, then, that African-American cinema and literature should create such loving, and mournful, epitaphs for fathers-brothers-sons, should be obsessed with the shadows which play out our wishes and dreams.

Notes

1. In his 1946 Introduction to *Black Metropolis*, Wright describes the life of the Negro in America as 'a small but a highly symbolically important part' of a fatal 'war of impulses' in 'the innermost heart of America' (Wright 1946b: xxi). That war of impulses was also, in 'How Bigger Was Born' (1940), described as symbolising the modern condition as such: if 'Modern man is afraid of himself and is at war with himself', in the alienated life of the Negro, Wright argued, the political affects of that internal war could be seen in all their alarming immediacy (ibid.: xxiii). In his '*snarled* and *confused* nationalist feelings', the postwar Negro was not only 'estranged from the religion and folk culture of his race', but was also 'trying to react to and answer the call of the dominant civilization which came to him', but from which he was excluded. Open to 'the potentialities of either Communism or Fascism', the basis of the Negro's social ties, according to Wright, are dictated by his emotional and

cultural hungers and fears, his hate and impatience, which leave him open to 'some gaudy, hysterical leader who'll promise rashly to fill the void in him', as well as the fraternal lure of worker's trade unions. Either way his 'feudal misery' will no longer support the *status quo*. The 'whirling vortex of [his] undisciplined and unchannelized impulses' lead Wright to 'feel more than ever estranged from the civilization in which I lived' (Wright 1983: 22).

2. I am indebted to Marie Balmary's discussion of Oedipus in *Psychoanalyzing Psychoanalysis: Freud and the Hidden Fault of the Father* (1982).
3. It should be said that Narcissus thought he was looking not at himself but at the image of a beloved: that is, it is a misrecognition which complicates the idea of narcissism as a simple turning round on self. The gendering of the narcissistic look in cinema was also a commonplace of the film theory on which Kennedy is drawing. See Lebeau 1995 and Mayne 1993 for an account of Laura Mulvey's classic sexing of the look and further discussion of the problem of the spectator in (feminist) film theory.
4. For Kennedy, too, the symbolic efforts of *Boyz* to 'counteract a sociological assertion – that of paternal abandonment', as featured in the Moynihan Report, results in a 'world of fathers and sons' being offered as a solution to the problems currently affecting black family life (Kennedy 1992: 110). The concern, here, that Afro-America is recognising itself through fantasmatic images of black masculinity on screen, seems to repeat, albeit negatively, George's presumption that 'most' African-Americans succumbed to, and were seduced by, something in the cinematic spectacle of *Boyz*.

Afterword: Either/Or

> *'what, what nigger?'* (The murderers of Stephen Lawrence, 10.25 p.m., 22 April 1993)

> In the Deep South they used to call this lynching. (Gary Younge, *Guardian*, 25 February 1999)

The photograph shows a casually dressed young black man looking directly at the camera wearing an enigmatic, teasing hint of a smile. It is the simplest sort of family photograph; capturing a moment of small reverie and intimate disclosure. You know about families and their snapshots. You know how children are pleaded with and cajoled into having their pictures taken for posterity. This photograph, like so many others, depicts a moment of family privacy, wrested from the outer world; the consensual, living presence of a son simultaneously masked and revealed by the eye of the camera. What you see is an ordinary event taken from an ordinary family's photograph album. There is nothing else to see. You scan the features briefly, then turn the page.

Over the next six years your perception of this image will change radically as you learn to see the breadth of its impact. You will see another moment exposed in this family drama or scene. It shows a boy bleeding to death from two fatal stab wounds in Eltham, South East London, his image – his death – seen by a distraught friend, concerned passers-by, and several contemptuous police officers. It is not just another racial murder. It is, some say, an image of a lynching superimposed on a private moment recorded by parents who thought they were doing something simple and tender, taking the picture of a beloved son. Some photographs blur and fade, wearing away at the edges. The persistence of this photo lies elsewhere – in the agonised, sometimes duplicitous, public conscience of white, middle England which has finally become aware of what it means to be young, black and male in contemporary Britain.

6.1 Stephen Lawrence. Copyright © Photo News Service.

But there is also an element of blindness. You keep on scanning this image not because you don't know the outcome of the boy's life, but precisely because you do. There is a crude and ominous power operating here. You keep on looking because things combine to hold you fast – a sense of the random, the arbitrary, the impending, and the preordained. You no longer think of the photo as a private memory but as a public spectacle and memorial emblem, tragic, blunt, relentless. It is the jostled part of your mind, the film that runs through all the thoughts you know you're thinking about other murdered black men, men intimate with dying, images that bring together photography and lynching. An unwitting kind of intimacy, to be sure, burdened and weary, tainted and cursed.

Lynching scenes are lurking in the camera, already framed, waiting for those five white youths who will come along and say '*what, what nigger?*', before plunging a knife in the boy's chest and arms to a depth of five inches, then running off into the night, screaming loudly, brave with their own recklessness. It shows a seated boy alone in a frame, waiting nervously for that unseen moment already haunting the eye of the camera. For you this photo is both a reproach and an accusation – regardless of where the blame is laid. His look addresses you without seeing you; it exposes what lies at the bottom of the racism infecting the abstract, liberal doctrine of rights and freedom before the law. And this is another reason why you keep on looking. The photograph has a searing realism amid the rehearsed media narratives of national shame and timely, political displays of unassuaged grief. Behind each dot you sense a deep catastrophe of memory, generation upon generation of lives obliterated and exposed, grainy and grey.

It shows him relaxed and happy to comply with the wish that his photograph be taken.

You know how families mourn their sons. This is just another family mourning the loss of a son tragically murdered while waiting for a bus. Doreen Lawrence, his mother, especially liked this photograph and so released it to the media. This is her son and she is aware of the intrusions of letting strangers see it but she wants them to feel her loss. This image, now omnipresent, carries her private memories of a bright, eighteen year old boy who was studying to become an architect. Her son.

And you keep on looking. You look because this is the nature of the image, to make a channelled path through time, to give life a memorial shape and a destiny. Of course, if Stephen hadn't persuaded his friend, Duwayne Brooks, to get off the number 286 and change buses at 10.25 p.m. on the evening of 22 April, that family photo would have remained inside its frame rather than purloined by a media frenzy. The chance quality of the encounter. The victim, those five killers and the spectacle, in 1999, of public institutions forced to confront the spectre of institutional racism. There's something surreal here that speaks to you directly, something shameful in the media coverage, lines of intersection which knowingly fail to reveal the essential conflicts at work – moments of acute public disavowal and symbolic confrontation which fully articulate the terms of this racial drama.

Stephen wandered into it. He got off the number 286 and wandered clear-eyed into horror. In *Why Stephen?*, one of the many factual programmes broadcast about his death, Charles Wheeler described Stephen's murder as a 'lynching'. This is a familiar story about straying too far from a culture's projected mirror-image of black men. It is not the camera that puts black men in the tale, but racial violence and murder. The media melodrama surrounding Stephen's death may be cheap, overwrought, and hollow, but it has also been a tellingly hyperbolic, lurid and grandiose event in its awareness that life in contemporary Britain has been distorted by a racial lens. His death, according to the *Guardian*'s leader comment, 'forced us all to take a long, uncomfortable look in the mirror, to examine not just the people we pay to protect us but ourselves' (25 February 1999). The true shadow cast by lynching – in that mirror – points to another history and logic underlying this murder, one hidden and masked. The site of Stephen's murder – a suburban bus stop in the white, working-class, overwhelmingly racist community of Eltham – and the fugitive, private way in which it was carried out, should not disallow this insight. In the press reactions written overwhelmingly by white men, Stephen's murder has become the repository of the fragmentary and desacralised remnants of conscience liberalism; a sphere where supposedly our most basic desires and interdictions lie, a realm in which our quotidian sense of moral decency may appear closed-off from us, but which we must accede to since it is the realm of meaning and value in being English. As if racism, in the words of Trevor Philips, could ever be 'a matter of individual likes and dislikes', a conviction to be decided by reasoned refusal, a moral dilemma to be brooded over with one's conscience, an affair of the heart too deep to be approached by any real sense of history, a question of sincerity to be decided alone (*Observer*, 28 February 1999).

You know about decency and respect for due process of law and how five white working-class, ill-educated thugs are depicted as evil villains while Stephen is a metaphor of virtue fallen and unrevenged. If you've seen his image many times you know that there is also no middle ground or condition between a promising life and brutal death. The bodies of black men have become a sort of moral emblem which must be sought for, postulated, and eradicated from existence by the vicious racism of young white men. When the five murderers of Stephen Lawrence looked across the street and saw a young black man, what they saw stationed in their path was a blurred but recognisable image veering toward them, a nonfictional legend to be combatted and expelled, witnessed and dispatched, steely and clear. After he'd fallen, desperate to breathe, and they'd run laughing down the street, they didn't even think of looking back, nor did they care.

You don't usually watch TV in the middle of the afternoon, especially the BBC's 24 hour cable news channel. You have your favourite programmes, and the news is not one of them. But there's an expectant urgency on the screen today. Waiting for the Lawrences' response to Sir William Macpherson's report into the killing of their son, you feel something is going to happen finally and you want to be there, to bear witness. They hold their press conference at the Home Office. The overcrowded room visibly jumps as they enter, as a mob of journalists and press photographers surges forward eager to capture them. After what looks like a pained, awkward pose for the photographers – the camera trained on them all the while – Neville Lawrence stands up and sits apart from his wife. At some level this gesture is delicate, unfailingly polite, but watching it, unprepared, you're seeing an absence appear between them which you know to be anchored in psychic pain.

Doreen Lawrence speaks first. Her voice is faltering, hesitant, as if overcome with the sheer weariness of it all – six years of grief, private prosecutions, police incompetence, public vilification and the wretchedness of knowing that the five men who killed her son are still walking free. '[A] woman worn out' is how the *Guardian* describes her on the front page 25 February 1999. That weariness is real – a reaction that brings a mixture of pity and awe into the frame, making you wonder about the emotional and psychological price of the last six years. She paints an image of black lives held cheap, of the risks involved in blacks existing in Britain, dying in custody and in police vans.

You sit there thinking about that image of Stephen, how unremarkable it seems. When the camera pans onto Neville and he has thanked his legal advisers and the Inquiry team, you realise now why you stay fixed to the screen. The Lawrences have been playing on a theatre that is the point of juncture, and clash, of racial imperatives beyond themselves, imperatives which are non-mediated and irreducible. Their performance has been instructional. It demonstrates an elemental truth, that every breath you take has a different value depending on whether you are white or black. Thinking of Stephen and his parents as unlucky victims may allow you to feel a little less guilty, but you already know that here, caught on camera, the Lawrences have revealed the relentless logic that killed him; that the life choices of whiteness and blackness are absolute and irremissable: either-or.

This is what TV-photography does. It peels back the shadows and exposes the despised and contested, the perpetrators and victims. It makes reality into a narrative, enlarged and repositioned inside the most mundane events. You don't know why you are watching this. Inside those shaming and exposed images, you feel empty and disappointed, almost spent. Yet, after the broadcast ends and the camera cuts back to the studio, you rewind the tape, slow it down, freeze frame the Lawrences posing for the photographers. There is a sequence – a logic? – to that image which exposes your obsession. There is regret, some irony, a certain pride and embarrassment, a touch of rueful, even mournful, self-reflection and so on. The dilemma of blackness mostly invisible, but now humanly visible inside a Home Office room.

The whole country has been engaged in the making and marking of this public portrayal. For you the faces of the Lawrences have simply become too compressed an image, covered over by compact fears and anger about the rights of individuals and of victims, familial and human rights, the laws of state. That image has become the centre for earnestly rehearsed and ever painful caricatures of young black men – visions of violent lawlessness that had figured early on in the police investigation into Stephen's death. It is something, this monochrome moralism, to which white residents of Eltham have clung in their belief that Stephen was involved either in gang war or a drugs conflict over turf. A monochrome image easily available from the media who would have used it but for the fact that Stephen's image was clearly not operable within the tropes, evocations, and discourses of a dangerous, black masculinity. The heightening and hyperbole, the polarised conflict, the menace and suspense of these representations shows an effort to perceive and image the class derelictions of white racism via some kind of manichean equation. These are indelible half-fictions impelled by one simple fact: the five prime suspects will never be brought to trial, the police have already seen to that. Knowing this, you also know that the power of racial abuse is not just a sign of pathology, or legal loophole, or failure in police procedure; it is fuelled by a culture and community of consent. The realms of the private and public spheres in Britain and America are permeated by the most pernicious racist fantasies which the press and broadcast media have been slow to address. Fantasies which converge on the uncanny resemblance between racist imagery and political interests.

You look at the TV screen: Neville Lawrence is nearing the point where he expresses his future hope that we can all go forward from Stephen's death; you wait for the tone of conviction but it never comes. You know this is not an invitation to despair. The days of mass lynchers escaping with impunity have surely gone, even though the law has invariably failed to understand the site of those private melodramas enacted in Eltham. Yesterday, on 24 February, the *Guardian* newspaper ran a front page detailing twenty five other racially motivated murders of black and Asian men that have taken place in England and Wales since 1991. You cut from that front page back to the frozen image of Neville Lawrence. You look back at those faces, half-mesmerised. The subjects are all overtly posing – their smiles belie what you know of their fates and the fatedness of these odd, mawkish photographs. They all seem so interchangeable, these juxtaposed images projected onto a screen bearing the headline, *And the racist killings go on*, a moral gesturing which strikes you as somewhat emotional, even didactic – the entire page strangely excessive, extreme, off-kilter and impressive all at the same time. You know that the pathologies of culture have always been reflected in the exercise of state power against blacks, and here is the proof. The camera eye fixed on the Lawrences is the same camera eye that itemised and recorded the inequities of those other murders as the debased sign of some ghetto melodrama. The same camera eye revealed recording more than a century of black death and suffering, painstakingly mimeographed and framed by the mutilated bodies of black men. Like you, those dead men peering from the page – from the screen – already understand what it means to say that the message is the medium.

As you lie awake at night seeing that repeated image of Stephen, you are literally shaken by foreboding. Every time you see the photograph you see one possible version of yourself in the picture. Watching yourself from the screen, or else seeing yourself bleeding copiously by the curb on Dickson Road, you realise your private life is out in the open, barely able to escape. A recognition of congruence and an evocation of superimposition, merged, twinned, and continued in a lifetime spent deciphering racist connotations and symbols. Stephen is displayed in newspaper photographs, he survives in the memories of his family, he remains a presence in your life and the lives of black people. He accompanies you wherever you are exposed to spectacles of black torture and humiliation, rites of white initiation, and the moral manicheanism of either-or. And why not? You know you could die just by changing a bus, by standing on a streetcorner, by walking outside the frame.

In his report, Sir William Macpherson spoke of the 'existence of a sub-culture of obsessive violence, fuelled by racist prejudice and hatred against black people, such as is exemplified in the 1994 video films of the five prime suspects'. He judged this to be 'a condemnation of them and also of our society' (cited in *The Times*, 25 February 1999). You turn off the TV. A series of images begins to fill the room. You see a long trail of blood framed like a silhouette that takes you hauntingly back to a memory of childhood and to an image framed and gleaming on the mantlepiece in the dark hall. You aren't able to identify or name the face of the boy looking out at you, as your eyes shift from the photographic surface to a memory locked in recall, the delicate visuals of a camera obscura, representing a clearing in the woods and a group of upturned faces studying what looks like the outline of an abnormal pall. Reflected in those faces you see the same image of a mutilating, deforming vision, the same yearning telemetry of crowds.

Brighton, 25 February 1999

Works Cited

Adler, Alfred (1908) 'The Aggression Drive', in H. L. Ansbacher and R. R. Ansbacher (eds), *The Individual Psychology of Alfred Adler: A Systematic Presentation In Selections from His Writings*, New York: Harper & Row, 1964.

Ali, Muhammad (1975) *The Greatest*, New York: Random House.

Bagehot, Walter (1875) *Physics and Politics: Or Thoughts on the Application of the Principles of 'Natural Selection' and 'Inheritance' to Political Society*, Henry S. King and Co., London.

Baldwin, James (1964) *Notes of a Native Son*, London: Michael Joseph.

—— (1965) *Going to Meet the Man*, London: Michael Joseph.

—— (1976) *The Devil Finds Work*, London: Michael Joseph.

—— (1976a) 'Interview with Inmates at Riker's Island Prison in New York,' in *Essence*, June.

—— (1991) *Nobody Knows My Name: More Notes of a Native Son*, Harmondsworth: Penguin.

—— (1998), *The Collected Essays*, New York: Library of America.

Baldwin, Mark (1895) *Mental Development in the Child and the Race*, New York: Macmillan.

Balmary, Marie (1982) *Psychoanalyzing Psychoanalysis: Freud and the Hidden Fault of the Father*, trans. Ned Lukacher, Baltimore and London: Johns Hopkins University Press.

Beam, Joseph (1986) *In the Life: A Black Gay Anthology*, Boston: Alyson Publications, Inc.

Benjamin, Walter (1985) *One Way Street and Other Writings*, trans. Edmund Jephcott and Kingsley Shorter, London and New York: Verso.

Blyden, Edward (1967) *Christianity, Islam and the Negro Race*, Edinburgh: Edinburgh University Press.

—— (1971) *Black Spokesmen: Selected published writings of Edward Wilmot Blyden*, London: Cass.

Bogle, Donald (1973) *Toms, Coons, Mulattoes, Mammies, and Bucks*, New York: Viking Press.

Brooks, Peter (1984) *Reading for the Plot: Design and Intention in Narrative*, Cambridge, MA and London: Harvard University Press.

Bulhan, H. A. (1985), *Frantz Fanon and the Psychology of Oppression*, New York: Plenum.

Cameron, James (1995) *A Time of Terror: A Survivor's Story*, London and New York: Writers and Readers, first edn 1982.

Celant, Germano (1992) 'The Satyr and the Nymph: Robert Mapplethorpe and his Photography', in *Mapplethorpe*, Hayward Gallery Catalogue: Electra.

Chamoisseau, Patrick (1996) *Childhood*, trans. Carol Volk, London: Granta.

Clark, Kenneth and Mamie Clark (1966) 'Racial Identification and Preference in Negro Children', in Eleanor E. Maccoby, Theodore M. Newcomb, and Eugene L. Hartley (eds), *Readings in Social Psychology*, London: Methuen, pp. 602–11.

Cripps, Thomas (1993) *Making Movies Black: The Hollywood Message Movie from World War II to the Civil Rights Era*, New York and Oxford: Oxford University Press.

Crummell, Alexander (1992) *Destiny and Race: Selected Writings, 1840–1898*, Wilson Jeremiah Moses (ed.), Amherst: University of Massachusetts Press.

——(1995) *Civilization and Black Progress: Selected Writings of Alexander Crummell on the South*, ed. J. R. Oldfield, Charlottesville, VA: University Press of Virginia.

Danto, Arthur C. (1996) *Playing with the Edge: The Photographic Achievement of Robert Mapplethorpe*, Berkeley: University of California Press.

Douglass, Frederick (1950) *The Life and Times of Frederick Douglass. 4 Volumes: Volume 1: Early Years, 1817–1849*, International Publishers.

Dowd, Jerome (1914) 'Discussion', appended to Ulysses G. Weatherly, 'The Racial Element in Social Assimilation', *The American Journal of Sociology*, pp. 593–635.

——(1927) 'The Psyche of the Negro', in *The Negro in American Life*, London: Jonathan Cape.

Dowd Hall, Jacqueline (1984) '"The Mind That Burns in Each Body": Women, Rape, and Racial Violence', in Ann Snitow, Christine Stansell and Sharon Thompson (eds.), *Desire: The Politics of Sexuality*, London: Virago, pp. 339–60.

Du Bois, W. E. Burghardt (1945) 'Richard Wright Looks Back', in John M. Reilly (ed.), *Richard Wright: The Critical Reception*, Burt Franklin & Co., Inc. [first appeared in *New York Herald Tribune Weekly Book Review*, 4 March 1945].

——(1992) 'Of Alexander Crummell', in Alexander Crummel, *Destiny and Race: Selected Writings, 1840–1898*, Wilson Jeremiah Moses (ed.), Amherst: University of Massachusetts Press, pp. 21–8.

Dyson, Michael Eric (1995) *Making Malcolm: the Myth and Meaning of Malcolm X*, Oxford: Oxford University Press.

Ellison, Ralph (1948) 'Harlem is Nowhere', in *Shadow and Act*, New York: Secker and Warburg, 1967.

——(1949) 'Shadow and Act', in *Shadow and Act*, New York: Secker and Warburg, 1967.

Fabre, Michel (1985) *The World of Richard Wright*, Jackson: University

Press of Mississippi.

——(1974) 'Fathers and Sons in James Baldwin's *Go Tell It on the Mountain*', in Keneth Kinnamon (ed.), *James Baldwin: A Collection of Critical Essays*, Englewood Cliffs, NJ: Prentice Hall, pp. 120–38.

——(1993) *The Unfinished Quest of Richard Wright*, trans. Isabel Barzun, Urbana and Chicago: University of Illinois Press.

Fanon, Frantz (1952) *Peau noire, masques blancs*, Paris: Éditions du Seuil.

——(1967) *Black Skin, White Masks*, trans. C. L. Markmann, New York: Grove Press.

——(1967a) *The Wretched of the Earth*, trans. Constance Farrington, Harmondsworth: Penguin.

——(1970) *Towards the African Revolution*, Harmondsworth: Penguin.

Fanon, Frantz and C. Geronimi (1956) 'Le T. A. T. chez les femmes musulmanes: Sociologie de la perception et de l'imagination', in *Congrès des médecins aliénistes et neurologistes de France et des pays de langue française*, 54th session, Bordeaux, 30 August–4 September, pp. 364–8.

Fanon, Frantz and François Tosquelles (1953) 'Sur un essai de réadaptation chez une malade avec épilepsie morphéique et troubles de charactère grave', in *Congrès des médecins aliénistes et neurologistes de France et des pays de langue française*, 51st session, Pau, 20–6 July , pp. 363–8.

Faucet, Jessie (1925) 'The Gift of Laughter', in Angelyn Mitchell (ed.), *Within the Circle: An Anthology of African American Literary Criticism from the Harlem Renaissance to the Present*, Durham and London: Duke University Press, 1994, pp. 45–50.

Fenichel, Otto (1935) 'The Scopophilic Instinct and Identification', in Hanna Fenichel and David Rappaport (eds), *The Collected Papers of Otto Fenichel*, First Series, London: Routledge and Kegan Paul, 1954, pp. 373–97.

Gabbard, K. and G. O. Gabbard (1987) *Psychiatry and the Cinema*, Chicago: University of Chicago Press.

Garrigues, Jean (1991) *Banania: Histoire D'Une Passion Française*, Paris: Editions du May.

Gates, Henry Louis Jr. (1988) 'The Trope of a New Negro and the Reconstruction of the Image of the Black', *Representations* 24, Fall, pp. 129–55.

George, N. (1994) *Buppies, B-Boys, Baps & Bohos: Notes on Post-Soul Black Culture*, New York: HarperPerennial.

——(1994a) *Blackface: Reflections on African-Americans and the Movies*, New York: HarperCollins.

Gilroy, P. (1993) 'It's a Family Affair', in *Small Acts: Thoughts on the Politics of Black Cultures*, London: Serpent's Tail.

Golb, Gerald N. (1987) 'The Forging of Mental Health Policy in America: World War II to New Frontier', *Journal of the History of Medicine and Allied Sciences* 42: 410–46.

Griggs, Sutton (1905) *The Hindered Hand: Or, The Reign of the Repressionist*, Nashville: The Orion Publishing Co.

Hale, Nathan G. Jr. (1995) *The Rise and Crisis of Psychoanalysis in the United*

States: Freud and the Americans, 1917–1985, New York and Oxford: Oxford University Press.

Hall, Stuart (1996) 'The After-life of Frantz Fanon? Why Now? Why *Black Skin, White Masks*?' in Alan Read (ed.), *The Fact of Blackness: Frantz Fanon and Visual Representation*, Seattle: Bay Press.

Hernton, Calvin (1969) *Sex and Racism in America*, New York: Grove Press.

Hirsch, David A. H. (1996) '"Dahmer's Effects": Gay Serial Killer Goes to Market', in Cary Nelson and Dilip Parameshwar Gaonkar (eds), *Disciplinarity and Dissent in Cultural Studies*, New York: Routledge, pp. 441–72.

Kardon, Janet (1988) 'Robert Mapplethorpe Interview', in *Robert Mapplethorpe: The Perfect Moment*, Philadelphia: Institute of Contemporary Art Catalogue.

Kennedy, L. (1992) 'The Body in Question', in G. Dent (ed.), *Black Popular Culture*, Seattle: Bay Press.

Kluger, Richard (1977) *Simple Justice: the history of Brown v. Board of Education and black America's struggle for equality*, London: Deutsch.

Lacan, Jacques (1984) *Les complexes familiaux*, Dijon: Navarin Editeur.

—— (1988) *The Seminar of Jacques Lacan. Book I: Freud's Papers on Technique 1953–1954*, J.-A. Miller (ed.), trans. John Forrester, Cambridge: Cambridge University Press.

—— (1988a) *The Seminar of Jacques Lacan. Book II: The Ego in Freud's Theory and in the Technique of Psychoanalysis 1954–1955*, J.-A. Miller (ed.), trans. S. Tomaselli, Cambridge: Cambridge University Press.

Lebeau, Vicky (1995) *Lost Angels: Psychoanalysis and Cinema*, London and New York: Routledge.

—— (1998) 'Psychopolitics: Frantz Fanon's *Black Skin, White Masks*', in J. Campbell and J. Harbord (eds), *Psycho-politics and Cultural Desires*, London: Taylor and Francis, pp. 113–23.

Locke, Alain (1925) 'The New Negro', in Angelyn Mitchell (ed.), *Within the Circle: An Anthology of African American Literary Criticism from the Harlem Renaissance to the Present*, Durham and London: Duke University Press, 1994, pp. 21–31.

Lynch, H. R. (1967) *Edward Wilmot Blyden: Pan-Negro Patriot*, 1832–1912, Oxford: Oxford University Press.

Mapplethorpe, Robert (1982) 'Interview with Gerritt Henry', *The Print Collector's Newsletter* (September–October): 129.

—— (1983) *Black Males*, Amsterdam: Gallerie Jurka.

—— (1986) *The Black Book*, Munich: Schirmer/Mosel.

Masters, Brian (1993) *The Shrine of Jeffrey Dahmer*, London: Hodder and Stoughton.

Mayne, Judith (1993) *Cinema and Spectatorship*, London and New York: Routledge.

McCall, N. (1994) *Makes Me Wanna Holler*, New York: Vintage Books.

Mecklin, J. M. (1914) *Democracy and Race Friction. A Study in Social Ethics*, New York: Macmillan Study.

Menil, René (1996) 'The Situation of Poetry in the Caribbean', in Michael Richardson (ed.), *Refusal of the Shadow: Surrealism and the Caribbean*, trans. Michael Richardson and Krzysztof Fijalkowski, London: Verso, pp. 127–34.

Mercer, Kobena (1994) *Welcome to the Jungle*, London: Routledge.

Miller, Warren (1949) 'Home of the Brave', *Masses and Mainstream*, 2 (July), 7: 79–82.

Mitchell, Angelyn (ed.) (1994) *Within the Circle: An Anthology of African American Literary Criticism from the Harlem Renaissance to the Present*, Durham and London: Duke University Press.

Morrisroe, Patricia (1995) *Mapplethorpe: A Biography*, London: Macmillan.

Moses, Wilson Jeremiah (1992) *Alexander Crummell: A Study of Civilisation and Discontent*, Amherst: University of Massachusetts Press.

Odum, Howard W. (1910) *Social and Mental Traits of the Negro*, New York and London: Columbia University Press (*Studies in History, Economics and Public Law Series*, Vol. xxxvii (37), No. 3).

Rainwater, Lee and William L. Yancey (1967) *The Moynihan Report and the Politics of Controversy*, Cambridge, MA and London: Harvard University Press.

Sartre, J.-P. (1969) *Being and Nothingness*, trans. Hazel E. Barnes, London: Routledge.

—— (1988) *'What is Literature?' and Other Essays*, Cambridge, MA: Harvard University Press.

Selzer, Mark (1998) *Serial Killers: Death and Life in America's Wound Culture*, London: Routledge.

Spencer, Herbert (1893) *Principles of Psychology*, 2 Volumes, London: William and Norgate.

Spillers, Hortense (1987) 'Mama's Baby, Papa's Maybe: An American Grammar Book', *Diacritics* 17, 2, pp. 65–81.

Staples, B. (1994) *Parallel Time: Growing Up in Black and White*, New York: Avon Books.

Steele, Shelby (1988) 'On Being Black and Middle-Class', *Commentary*, January.

Stepto, Robert (1979) *From Behind the Veil*, Urbana: University of Illinois Press.

Sterba, Richard (1947) 'Some Psychological Factors in Negro Race Hatred and in Anti-Negro Riots', *Psychoanalysis and the Social Sciences* I, pp. 411–27.

Taylor, Patrick (1989) *The Narrative of Liberation: Perspectives on Afro-Caribbean Literature, Popular Culture, and Politics*, Ithaca: Cornell University Press.

Tyre, Nedra (1947) *Red Wine First*, New York: Simon and Schuster.

Wallace, M. (1992) 'Boyz N the Hood and Jungle Fever', in G. Dent (ed.), *Black Popular Culture*, Seattle: Bay Press.

Weatherly, Ulysses G. (1916) 'The Racial Element in Social Assimilation', *The American Journal of Sociology* XVI: 593–612.

Wells-Barnett, Ida B. (1991) *Selected Works of Ida B. Wells-Barnett*, New York: Oxford University Press, first edn 1895.

Wideman, John Edgar (1994) *Fatheralong: A Meditation on Fathers and Sons, Race and Society*, New York: Pantheon Books.

Wright, Richard (1935) 'Between the World and Me', *Partisan Review* 2 (July–August): 19.

——(1945) *Black Boy: A Record of Childhood and Youth*, New York and Evanston: Harper & Row.

——(1945a) 'How Richard Wright Looks at Black Boys', *PM* 15 April, pp. 3–4.

——(1946) 'Introduction', Horace R. Cayton and St. Clair Drake, *Black Metropolis*, London: Jonathan Cape, pp. xvii–xxxiv.

——(1947) *Twelve Million Black Voices: A Folk History of the Negro in the United States of America*, London: Lindsay Drummond, first edn 1941.

——(1947a) 'How Jim Crow Feels', *Negro Digest*, January, pp. 44–55.

——(1954) *Black Power: A Record of Reactions in a Land of Pathos*, New York: Harper.

——(1977) *American Hunger*, New York: Harper.

——(1983) *Native Son*, Harmondsworth: Penguin.

Index

Ali, Muhammad, 22n

Bagehot, Walter, 52
Baldwin, James
'Alas, Poor Richard', 106–7
on cinema, xiii, 92n
'Going to Meet the Man', 15–20
and Richard Wright, 105–9
Baldwin, Mark, 50
Beam, Joseph, vii, 99
Black Nationalism *see* Crummell, Alexander
Blyden, Edward, 43, 44, 45, 63n
Christianity, Islam and the Negro Race, 56–8
Boyz N the Hood, 109–15
Brooks, Peter, 95
Burke, Edmund, 53, 64n

Cameron, James
A Time of Terror, 1–23
see also lynching; photography
castration, 6, 9, 14–15
and scopophilic instinct, 27, 32
Cripps, Thomas, 75
Crummell, Alexander
on black men as imitators, 47–9 *et passim*
and Edward Blyden, 44, 45, 56–8, 63n
'The Destined Superiority of the Negro', 52–6
and Frederick Douglass, 43, 44, 46, 63–4n
and W. E. B. Du Bois, 58–9
on mulattoes, 47, 49–50, 63
'Our National Mistakes and the Remedy for Them', 47–9
'The Need of New Ideas and New Aims for a New Era', 63–4n
'The Progress and Prospects of the Republic of Liberia', 45
and race psychology, 47, 50, 52, 53–6
on racial types, 43–4, 48–51
'The Social Principle among a People and Its Bearing on Their Progress', 51–2

Dahmer, Jeffrey, 34–41
Danto, Arthur C., 23–8
Delany, Martin, 45
Douglass, Frederick, 43, 58, 63–4
and 'Douglass Dictum', 46
Dowd, Joseph, 47, 50
on black psychology, 62–3
Du Bois, W. E. B., 103
The Souls of Black Folk, 58–9
Dyson, Michael Eric, 112

Ellison, Ralph
on Hollywood cinema, 74–5
relationship to Richard Wright, 93–4n, 104–5
'The Way It Is', 86
'The World and the Jug', 104, 105

Fabre, Michel, 108
Fanon, Frantz, viii, ix, x
on black *ressentiment*, 82–3
Black Skin, White Masks, 66–9 *et passim*
on cinema, 68–9, 76–9
critique of Freudian theory of the dreamwork, 91n
and Jacques Lacan, 80–1

on Kantian ethics, 87, 89
on racial misrecognition, 82–5
relationship to psychoanalysis, 66–7, 68, 70–1, 80–1, 89
revision of Hegelian ontology, 67, 70, 88, 90n
and Jean-Paul Sartre, 86–7
Toward the African Revolution, 85
on trauma and fantasy, 12–14, 66–7, 91–2n
on war, 66–7, 69–70 *et passim*
and Richard Wright, 86–7, 93n
fantasy
and fetishism, 12, 29, 30
and negrophobia, 10–11, 12, 68
and photography, 23–5 *et passim*
Faucet, Jessie, 61
Fenichel, Otto, 27, 41
Foreman, Carl, 75
fratricide, 109–15
Freud, Sigmund, 25–6, 71, 72, 91

Gates, H. L., 59–60
George, Nelson, 98, 110, 111
Gilroy, Paul, 111–12
Gobineau, Count de, 47
Griggs, Sutton, 10
Grinker, John, 72

Hegel, Georg, 67, 70, 88, 90n
Hernton, Calvin
Sex and Racism in America, 14–15
Home of the Brave, 70, 72–9, 86
Howe, Irving, 104

imago *see* Fanon, Frantz
imitation *see* Crummell, Alexander
incorporation
the scopophilic instinct and, 27

Julien, Isaac, 30

Kant, Immanuel, 89
Kennedy, Lisa, 110–11, 116
Kluge, Alexander, 111
Kramer, Stanley, 72, 75

Lacan, Jacques, 80
Lawrence, Stephen, 117–24
Lebeau, Vicky, 13
Lee, Spike, 110
Locke, Alain, 59–60

lynching, 1–23 *et passim*
see also photography

Mapplethorpe, Robert
Hooded Man, 30–2
Man in Polyester Suit, 25–7, 30–4
racial fetishism and, 28–9
X Portfolio, 23–5
Masters, Brian, 37
Mecklin, J. M., 47, 61–2n
Ménil, René, 83
Mercer, Kobena, 28–30, 32–3
Miller, Warren, 78
Moynihan Report, The, 98

narcosynthesis, 72–4, 92
see also *Home of the Brave*
negrophobia, 12–13
New Negro, The, 59–61
Nietzsche, Friedrich, x, 83

paternity
in African-American cinema, 109–12
black father-son relationships and, 95–115
fratricide and, 109–15,
Wideman, *Fatheralong*, 95–9, 114–15
photography
and lynching, 1–23
and fantasy, 23–5
psychiatry
and cinema, 72–3

Robson, Mark, 72

Sartre, Jean-Paul, 80, 86
scopophilia *see* Fenichel, Otto
Seltzer, Mark, 36
Singleton, John, 109
see also *Boyz N the Hood*
Spencer, Herbert, 47, 48
Spiegel, Roy, 72
Sterba, Richard, 91–2n

Till, Emmett, 22n
types
black men as, 43–63 *et passim*
Tyre, Nedra, 9

Wallace, Michelle, 110
war neuroses, 71
Wells-Barnett, Ida B.
A Red Record, 6, 9

Wideman, John Edgar
Fatheralong, 95–9, 114–15 *et passim*
see also paternity
Wright, Richard
'Between the World and Me', 5
Black Boy, 10–11, 99–101
Black Metropolis, 103, 115n
Black Power, vii, x, xi–xiii
'How Bigger Was Born', viii, 93–4n, 115n
'How Jim Crow Feels', 102
Native Son, 86, 87–8
relationship to James Baldwin, 105–9
on Southern family romance, 101–4
Twelve Million Black Voices, 6, 11